For Terry, with love.

Acknowledgements

Grateful thanks are due to: Paula Good, Assistant Press Officer at Ordnance Survey; Dave Matthews, Commercial Officer at Stagecoach Midland Red; Natashia Reeves, Publicity and Promotions Officer at Gloucestershire County Council and Jane Rollins, Public Relations Manager at National Express.

This book has been compiled in accordance with the *Guidelines for Writers of Path Guides* published by the Outdoor Writers' Guild.

DISCOVERY WALKS
in the
COTSWOLDS

Julie Meech

Published by Sigma Leisure – an imprint of
Sigma Press, 1 South Oak Lane, Wilmslow, Cheshire SK9 6AR, England.

British Library Cataloguing in Publication Data
A CIP record for this book is available from the British Library.

ISBN: 1-85058-634-9

Typesetting and Design by: Sigma Press, Wilmslow, Cheshire.

Cover photographs: Naunton, Vineyard Street; Winchcombe, Broadway Tower *(Julie Meech)*

Maps: Elizabeth Fowler

Text photographs: Julie Meech

Printed by: MFP Design and Print

Contents

The Walks

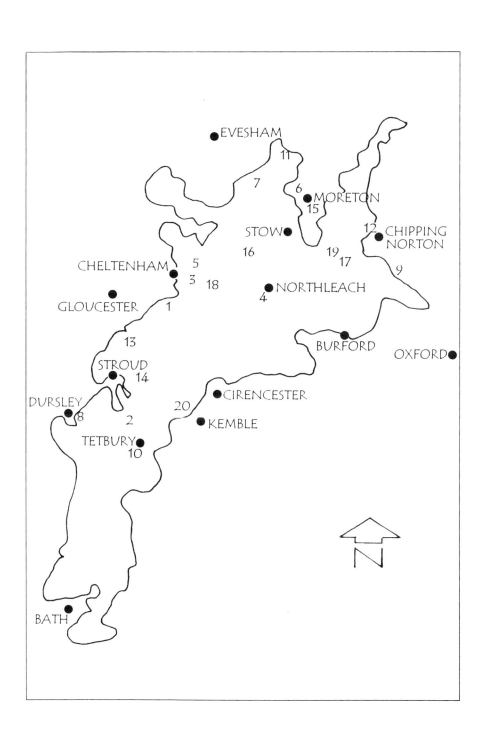

Introducing The Cotswolds

In H.J. Massingham's classic *Cotswold Country*, first published in 1937, the author writes about the limestone belt which stretches from the Dorset coast to Lincolnshire. Few of us today would define Cotswold in quite such wide terms, but exactly where we do draw the line is difficult to say. Strangers to the area must often feel confused when consulting the surprising number of guidebooks which claim to be about the Cotswolds but include such obviously un-Cotswold destinations as Gloucestershire's Severn Vale, Oxfordshire's Cherwell Valley or Worcestershire's Vale of Evesham.

If we take the officially designated Cotswold Area of Outstanding Natural Beauty as a guide then we must conclude that the Cotswolds stretch from Bath in Somerset to Edge Hill in Warwickshire, encompassing an area of 790 square miles (2038 sq. km.), the largest AONB in England and Wales. But when it was first designated in 1966 it covered a smaller area than this, and was only extended in 1991 – so perhaps officialdom isn't too sure either.

What seems to be most generally accepted as the Cotswolds is an area which roughly corresponds with the AONB and which sprawls over six counties – Gloucestershire, Oxfordshire, Worcestershire, Warwickshire, Wiltshire and Somerset - but with the lion's share overwhelmingly in Gloucestershire – "the high tide of the limestone country" as Massingham described it. The other main player is Oxfordshire, and the remaining counties are very much on the fringe, so much so that I have excluded Somerset and Wiltshire completely from this book, while Worcestershire and Warwickshire only just creep in. This is arbitrary, and many will not agree, but in an area where the borders are so fluid it must come down to personal choice in the end and there is little in Wiltshire or Somerset that feels Cotswold to me.

While my definition of Cotswold may be narrower than some, it still covers a huge area, but one with an amazing unity of character, despite the variety of different landscape types it embraces. It's the stone that defines it, the stone that has shaped everything: the form and texture of the land, the flowers and trees that thrive on it and the use that man has made of it. The stone, a type of oolitic limestone, lies close to the surface and is soft when first exposed, making it easily quarried and producing thin soils more suited to sheep than cereals. So Stone Age man was able to make his mark on the landscape by building some of the finest chambered stone tombs in England, and, centuries later, medieval merchants grew fat on the wool trade. They repaid their debt by building the incomparable "wool churches" which grace so many of the enchanting stone towns which characterise Cotswold still. Routinely described as "honey-coloured", the stone is actually extremely variable in colour, yet its ubiquitous use helps to unify this region which sprawls so widely. Nowhere else in England is there such a harmonious relationship between buildings and landscape, and it is this that makes Cotswold unique.

The "wool churches" are among the grandest buildings in the Cotswold scene, but the ordinary cottages, which seem almost to grow out of the landscape, are more characteristic. It was the stone which determined their shape and form, too. Having found a style of building in the Middle Ages which was ideally suited to the local stone, the Cotsallers stuck with it, for several generations and for all types of house. Until the classical revival of the 18th century the only significant differences between the largest mansions and the smallest cottages were those of scale. This means that houses in the region are not so much Tudor or Jacobean or Georgian as *Cotswold*, a distinct local vernacular which imposes a unity of style throughout.

Wherever you go you will find this same basic style in evidence: the steeply pitched roofs, for instance, which mean rainwater does not lie long enough to seep through the porous limestone, the carved drip moulds, the mullioned windows and the dormers and gables. All of these are features which evolved in response to local needs, local conditions, local skills and local stone.

To understand why so many of these houses have survived we must go back to the wool trade again. For centuries it brought prosperity but was eventually eclipsed by the cloth industry which flourished in the Stroudwater Hills, where fast-flowing streams and large deposits of fuller's earth provided ideal conditions for the development of mill towns. But Cotswold lacked cheap coal, and with the Industrial Revolution and the advent of coal-fired steam power the Pennines proved more than a match for the Cotswold towns, which simply could not compete. Economic stagnation set in, thus preventing the large-scale development and urbanisation which characterised so much of 19th-century Britain. Cotswold landscape and architecture remained predominantly unspoilt, poised to take advantage of the burgeoning tourist trade of the 20th century. This has brought its own problems, of course, with traffic congestion and the subsequent provision of bypasses and upgraded roads paramount amongst them. At the same time, so-called "attractions" have mushroomed and at least one Cotswold village has embraced tourism so wholeheartedly that few countrylovers would now wish to set foot in it. Cotswold has also become a desirable place to live or to own a weekend cottage, especially since the M4 was opened, and this has meant much new development and a creeping suburbanisation which has already destroyed the spirit and atmosphere of many a village. But these are problems which beset most of Britain, and there is still in Cotswold an enormous amount to admire and enjoy. The walks in this book seek to avoid what is worst about the region, and help you to discover much of what is best about it.

Long-Distance Paths and Other Designated Routes

Long-distance paths and other specially designated and waymarked routes have proliferated in recent years and Cotswold has more than its fair share. All the routes listed below are encountered, however briefly, in the walks described in this book, so a short summary may be helpful.

Centenary Way: 100 miles/160km; a linear walk through Warwickshire, from Kingsbury Water Park to Meon Hill, established in 1989 to celebrate the 100th anniversary of Warwickshire County Council.

Cotswold Way: 100 miles/160km; a linear walk from Chipping Campden to Bath which keeps mainly to the crest of the escarpment, providing great walking and fine views. Unusually for a long-distance path, it passes through, rather than round, towns and villages, emphasising the importance of the built landscape in Cotswold. Established in 1970, it was given National Trail status in February 1998.

Donnington Way: 62 miles/99km; a circular walk linking pubs serving real ale brewed at Donnington Brewery. The recommended starting point is Stow-in-the-Wold.

Gloucestershire Way: 100 miles/160km; a linear walk from Chepstow through the Forest of Dean, across the Severn Vale to the Cotswolds and then back to the Vale to end in Tewkesbury. Conceived on the theme of "Forest and vale and high blue hill" from the poem *A Song of Gloucestershire* by Will Harvey.

Heart of England Way: 100 miles/160km; a linear walk from Milford on the edge of Cannock Chase in Staffordshire to Bourton-on-the-Water.

Macmillan Way: 290 miles/464km; a linear walk along the limestone belt from Boston in Lincolnshire to Abbotsbury on the Dorset coast. Dedicated to the memory of Douglas Macmillan, the founder of the organisation now known as Cancer Relief Macmillan Fund. The walk has been developed to increase public awareness and to assist in fund-raising.

Monarch's Way: 610 miles/976km; a linear walk (by an indirect route) from Worcester to Shoreham which attempts to trace the approximate route taken by Charles II in fleeing the country after the Battle of Worcester in 1651.

North Cotswold Diamond Way: 60 miles/96km; a circular walk through the North Cotswolds established to celebrate the Ramblers' Association's Diamond Jubilee in 1995. Moreton-in-Marsh is the recommended starting point.

Oxfordshire Way: 65 miles/104km; a linear walk from Bourton-on-the-Water to Henley-on-Thames, connecting the Cotswolds to the Chilterns.

Thames Path: 180 miles/288km; a linear walk (and a National Trail) which follows the Thames (wherever possible) from the river's source near Kemble to the Thames Barrier in London's Docklands.

Wardens' Way: 13½ miles/22km; a linear walk linking Winchcombe with Bourton-on-the-Water via the villages of Upper and Lower Slaughter, Naunton and Guiting Power.

Windrush Way: 13½ miles/22km; a linear walk linking Winchcombe with Bourton-on-the-Water via the high wold. The two walks above were established by the Cotswold Voluntary Wardens and together they provide an interesting cross-section of Cotswold landscapes. Each can be tackled as a one-day linear walk or the two together can be treated as a two-day circular walk, with a night spent at either Bourton or Winchcombe.

Wychavon Way: 42 miles/67km; a linear walk from Holt Fleet in Worcestershire's Severn Valley to Winchcombe.

Some Practicalities

It's perhaps worth mentioning that the region should be referred to either as Cotswold or the Cotswolds, but not as the Cotswold Hills. Nor, except around Stroud, is it particularly hilly in the conventional sense. The main landscape feature is the upland wold, broken by numerous valleys, which rises almost imperceptibly from the Oxfordshire plain to culminate in a dramatic scarp slope which falls away steeply to the Severn Vale. It's not challenging walking country, though the high wold can be unexpectedly bleak, cheerless and remote-seeming, far removed from the rosy, cosy images of pretty villages which decorate much of the promotional material aimed at the general tourist. Even in the bleakest areas, however, you're never very far from houses, farms, shops, pubs or roads. The terrain is unlikely to pose any problem for most walkers as Cotswold never attains any great height and although there are plenty of steep slopes (Breakheart Hill near Dursley is well-named), none of them is sustained for more than a few hundred metres. The walks in this book, therefore, though they vary considerably both in length and in effort required, are not likely to prove beyond the capabilities of anyone of average fitness. However, they have been arranged in order of length, starting with the shortest, so if you do have any doubts about your stamina start at the beginning and work your way through.

It's as well to be properly equipped, although there's no need to invest in the sort of outrageously expensive gear which has recently become so trendy. Common sense is the best guide, which means taking waterproofs with you, and sufficient layers of warm clothing in winter. It's better not to wear jeans if rain threatens as they're uncomfortable when wet and very slow to dry. Proper walking boots are not necessary for all the walks in this book, especially in summer, but they do provide good ankle support, and they keep your feet dry in wet or muddy conditions (all the walks are potentially very muddy in winter) so it's often a good idea to wear them if you have them. They don't have to be the top-of-the-range type which leaves little change from £150. Entirely excellent boots can still be had for considerably less than that.

A small rucksack is the best way of carrying spare gear, but this doesn't have to be an expensive, highly specified affair either – you can get an adequate one for a few pounds. There are places to buy refreshment on all of the walks but it's still a good idea to carry food and drink with you, especially on the longer, more demanding ones. But don't carry too much weight, whether it's food, spare clothes or whatever; overburdening yourself is the surest way to get tired.

It can't be stressed too strongly how invaluable OS maps are. The directions in this book should ensure you don't get lost, but maps can tell you so much more: they enable you to make changes to the given route, to identify distant hills and to put the local scene in context. Maps contain an astonishing amount of information and, with a bit of practice, you can learn to read a map almost in the same way you might read a book. Landrangers (pink covers) are fine for an overview, but the large-scale Pathfinders (green covers) and Explorers (orange covers) are ideal for walkers. Superb companions on any excursion into the countryside, they help you to identify puzzling landscape features, such as prehistoric cultivation terraces or deserted medieval villages, and their tremendous level of detail makes route-finding easy, even showing which side of a hedge a footpath runs. The Pathfinder series is currently being replaced by the new Explorers, each of which covers a larger area, and the first Cotswold ones will be available in summer 1998, so keep your eyes open for the bright orange covers appearing in the shops. There is also a new Outdoor Leisure map (45) for the Cotswolds, first published in spring 1998, which covers many of the walks in this book.

The directions should enable you to complete the walks without any difficulty but bear in mind that things do change in the countryside – trees get blown over, hedges get ripped out, stiles may be replaced by gates or vice versa – any of which can cause confusion in route-finding. Please note that where the text indicates something along the lines of "climb a stile and go diagonally right", this assumes that, having climbed the stile, you are standing with your back to it. Footpaths get diverted too, but at least when this happens the new route is usually clearly waymarked. In fact, most footpaths in the Cotswolds are now fully waymarked anyway, with yellow arrows for footpaths and blue arrows for bridleways. The standard of rights of way maintenance is very high, thanks to the work of the Cotswold Voluntary Wardens, the volunteer arm of the Cotswold

Countryside Service. There are over 200 volunteer wardens, directed by full-time management staff. As well as maintaining rights of way, their work includes undertaking conservation schemes, devising and leading guided walks and providing information. The warden service is based at the Shire Hall in Gloucester.

Any obstructions or other problems pertaining to rights of way should be reported to the rights of way officer of the relevant county council or to the Cotswold Countryside Service at Shire Hall, Gloucester GL1 2TN (tel. 01452 425674).

Gloucestershire Wildlife Trust

A number of GWT nature reserves are encountered in the course of these walks and many readers might like to know more about the trust, which manages 80 nature reserves, provides environmental education to over 5000 schoolchildren every year, protects the best areas of wildlife in the county (monitoring over 900 identified Key Wildlife Sites) and encourages everyone to enjoy and care for local wildlife. It is a local charity working to protect the wildlife on our doorsteps, but, with Wildlife Watch, the environmental action club for children, it is also part of a national network of county wildlife trusts working to protect wildlife throughout the UK.

New members are always needed and membership benefits include six free magazines each year to keep you in touch with local and national issues, including the trust's own award-winning magazine and the national magazine *Natural World*. GWT's nature reserve handbook is a mine of information about the reserves, some of which are open only to members. There's no better way to discover more about your local countryside than to join your local wildlife trust. As well as the obvious benefits of discovering marvellous nature reserves, trust members also have opportunities to enjoy talks, training courses, a regular programme of events and the chance both to volunteer and to socialise. Gloucestershire Wildlife Trust is based at Dulverton Building, Robinswood Hill Country Park, Reservoir Road, Gloucester GL4 6SX. Telephone 01452 383333, fax 01452 383334, e-mail gmcg@cix.compulink.co.uk, web site http://www.wildlifetrust.org.uk/gloucestershire.

The Woodland Trust

In the course of Walk 17 you will also discover a Woodland Trust nature reserve, Trigmoor Wood near Kingham. The Woodland Trust is a national charity which acquires, conserves and creates woodlands, and, like the county wildlife trusts, it always welcomes new members. Virtually all Woodland Trust woods are open to the general public but if you want to know where they are, rather than simply stumbling on an occasional one by chance, you need the annual directory of properties which is sent free to members of the trust, who also receive regular newsletters. The Woodland Trust is based at: Autumn Park, Dysart Road, Grantham, Lincolnshire NG31 6LL. Telephone 01476 581111.

Countryside Stewardship

In the course of a few walks in this book you will encounter areas of countryside which are part of the Countryside Stewardship scheme. Administered by MAFF, this offers payments to farmers and landowners to enhance and conserve English landscapes, their wildlife and history. Agreements usually run for 10 years, and while public access is not a requirement, it is encouraged. All the Countryside Stewardship sites you will discover while doing these walks have public access and you are free to explore them. There are notices and detailed maps showing permitted access areas and footpaths at the entry point to each site.

Tourist Information Centres

Broadway (summer only) tel. 01386 852937

Burford tel. 01993 823558

Cheltenham tel. 01242 522878

Chipping Campden tel. 01386 841206

Chipping Norton tel. 01608 644379

Cirencester tel. 01285 654180

Gloucester tel. 01452 421188

Moreton-in-Marsh tel. 01608 650881

Northleach (summer only) tel. 01451 860715

Stow-on-the-Wold tel. 01451 831082

Stroud tel. 01453 765768

Tetbury (summer only) tel. 01666 503552

Winchcombe (summer only) tel. 01242 602925

There are also Tourist Information Points at:

Nailsworth tel. 01453 832532

Painswick tel. 01452 813552

Wotton-under-Edge tel. 01453 521451

Public Transport

And finally, in this introductory section, a plea for the environment. Instead of travelling around the Cotswolds by car, how about giving public transport a go? Anybody who regularly walks in the countryside must be aware of how difficult it is to escape the sight and sound of traffic. There's hardly a view not blighted by it, nor a village not choked by it, while the constant roar drowns out all the noises of the natural world. Major new road schemes violate the landscape while intrusive traffic signs and car parks dominate once-beautiful towns and villages. Other road users (pedestrians, cyclists, horse riders, pets and wildlife) are subject to increasing hazards on hitherto quiet country lanes, while some rural villages are resorting to ugly urban traffic-calming measures to try and ensure the safety of their children. This visual and aural pollution is all too apparent; less obvious but potentially more dangerous is the air pollution caused by the 36 billion gallons of poisonous fumes which Britain's vehicles belch out every day. With the Countryside Commission predicting a doubling, or even trebling, of rural traffic, it can only get worse. It's ironic that people talk of spending time in the countryside to find "peace and quiet" and "to get away from it all" and yet they go there by car, thereby helping to destroy the very thing they're in search of, and providing ammunition for the arguments of those who would build yet more bypasses. And ironic too, that for many of these visitors their main reason for being there is to walk.

Most people see the car as their only travel option, but it's just one of several options. It's perfectly possible to get around on public transport. I've been exploring the Cotswolds by bus, train and leg-power since 1985 and all the walks in this book were reached by public transport. It's not just environmentally friendly, it's also, believe it or not, easy, cheap and fun. Of course, many services are desperately in need of improvement, but we get the public transport we deserve. If we use it, the demand will encourage the provision of more and better services. If we don't use it, we'll lose it altogether.

Trains

Access by train is easy, with two important rail lines (Cheltenham/Gloucester to Swindon/Paddington and Hereford/Worcester to Oxford/Paddington) slicing through the Cotswolds. The Gloucester to Bristol line also provides some access, with a station at Cam and Dursley (and another at Yate for visitors to the Southwolds – beyond the scope of this book). The Cotswold Line between Worcester and Oxford is particularly useful, not just because it has several stations along its length, but also because the main operator, Thames Trains, is well aware of the potential market offered by walkers and has developed a number of valuable initiatives, from simple walks leaflets to the provision, in conjunction with Castleways Coaches, of a special bus service. The Cotswold Explorer (Castleways 569) operates daily except for winter Sundays, linking the rail stations at Evesham and Moreton-in-Marsh with such popular destinations as Broadway, Chipping Campden, Blockley and Batsford Arboretum. Integrated ticketing is now available - pay a little extra for your rail ticket and you can use it for travel on several Cotswold bus services. Just ask for "Cotswold Bus" when you buy your train ticket.

All Cotswold Line ticket holders (any ticket) enjoy reduced admission prices and discounts at a variety of venues, ranging from restaurants to river trips, from museums to stately homes, and also on cycle hire at Moreton. Pick up a leaflet at most Cotswold Line stations to find out where discounts are available and then just show your rail ticket to qualify. Anybody planning to travel regularly on the line should buy the annual Network Card to obtain a one-third reduction on off-peak fares. Thames Trains publishes free pocket timetables, available at manned stations, which include the times of connecting buses and details of guided walks from Cotswold Line stations, arranged and led by the Cotswold AONB Service.

There have been numerous improvements on the line in recent years, many of which have been due to the efforts of the Cotswold Line Promotion Group. Membership gets you regular newsletters, opportunities for social occasions and special charter trains and keeps you up to date with developments affecting the line. The larger the membership the more CLPG can press for service improvements, so if you'd like to join send a SAE to Mr J.E. Stanley, Membership Secretary, 4 Sandford Rise, Charlbury, Oxon OX7 3SZ. Alternatively, you can ring Oliver Lovell, the Promotions Officer, on 01608 650968.

National Express Coaches

Many people will be aware that National Express, with its low fares and high level of reliability, also offers a good way to reach the Cotswolds from all parts of the country. But what fewer people realise is that National Express can also be a good way to travel on relatively short journeys within the region, not just to and from it. A number of services operating via Gloucester and Cheltenham also call at places such as Charlton Kings, Stroud, Cirencester and Northleach. Also extremely useful is the 511 which operates daily between Great Malvern and London, calling at Evesham, Broadway, Moreton, Chipping Norton, Enstone and Woodstock. National Express services operating to Cotswold destinations include the 332, 335, 337, 339, 347, 503, 511 and 512.

Local Buses

Fun and friendly, local buses are still very numerous and will get you to most corners of Cotswold, far beyond the places which can be penetrated by trains or long-distance coaches. Some routes have services every few minutes, while others tend to be of the "second Wednesday in every other month" variety. On the whole, however, services are better than you might expect and look likely to improve further now that National Trail status has been confirmed for the Cotswold Way - the package of planned improvements includes more money for buses. Fares can be astonishingly low, especially with the smaller companies, and reliability is hard to fault. It's well worth investigating the wide range of rover and explorer tickets on offer: Stagecoach, for instance, has many different ones available to suit different needs. They all offer superb value for money.

Transport Information

Information about public transport is easy to obtain. Local authorities operate enquiry lines and produce timetable leaflets which may be picked up at bus and rail stations, travel centres, libraries and tourist information centres, or obtained direct from the councils. Individual travel operators have their own enquiry lines and most publish timetables. In addition, many libraries, tourist information centres, travel centres, bus stations and rail stations have copies of the National Rail Timetable, the National Express Timetable and the Great Britain Bus Timetable, which includes virtually all inter-urban and rural bus services in Britain plus details of rail interchange. Also available on subscription, it's published thrice-yearly by Southern Vectis Bus Company, Nelson Road, Newport, Isle of Wight PO30 1RD. Telephone 01983 522456.

Another useful source of information is the Countrygoer project. Annual membership gets you four issues of *Countrygoer News*, and copies of *Countrygoer Travel Guide* and *Scenic Britain by Bus*. Write to Countrygoer at 15 Station Road, Knowle, Solihull, West Midlands B93 0HL or call 01564 771901.

Train and coach timetables normally change twice a year, but local bus services are subject to more frequent change and it is always advisable to check before travelling, by calling either the relevant county travel enquiry line or the bus company involved. The relevant local authority numbers are:

Gloucestershire tel. 01452 425543 (0745-1700 Monday to Friday)

Oxfordshire tel. 01865 810405 (not actually a dedicated enquiry line but information can usually be obtained on this number during office hours)

South Gloucestershire, Bath and NE Somerset tel. 0117 955 5111 (0800-2000 daily)

Warwickshire, tel. 01926 414140 (0830-1730 Monday to Thursday, 0830-1700 Friday)

Wiltshire tel. 0345 090899 (0800-1800 Monday to Friday)

Worcestershire tel. 0345 125436 (0800-1900 Monday to Friday, 0900-1700 weekends)

There are too many local bus companies to list them all, but a small selection of the most useful ones for the purposes of this book includes:

Barry's Coaches tel. 01608 650876

Castleways Coaches tel. 01242 602949

Pulham's Coaches tel. 01451 820369

Stagecoach Cheltenham and District tel. 01242 522021

Stagecoach Gloucester Citybus tel. 01452 527516

Stagecoach Midland Red tel. 01788 535555

Stagecoach Stroud Valleys tel. 01453 763421

Swanbrook tel. 01452 712386

Other useful numbers include:

National Express tel. 0990 808080 (0800-2000 daily)

National Rail Enquiries tel. 0345 484950 (24 hours)

TBC (train, bus and coach) Hotline tel. 0891 910910 (0600-2100 daily)

For public transport information on the Internet log on to UK Public Transport Information at http://www.compulink.co.uk/-aus--an/ptinfo/

Walk 1: Cranham Corner to Brockworth

A short and very easy linear walk with no stiles to cross, which gives a brief introduction to the beautiful Cotswold beechwoods. The walk as described here ends either at Brockworth or on the A46 (Cheltenham to Stroud bus route) but can easily be turned into a circular walk if preferred, without adding more than a few hundred metres to the length.

Start: Cranham Corner, on the A46 north of Painswick, grid reference 882130.

Finish: Ermin Street (A417), Brockworth, grid reference 891164.

Length: 4½ miles/7.2km.

Maps: OS Landrangers 162 and 163, OS Pathfinder 1089.

Refreshments: Pubs at Cranham Corner (about 300 metres south of starting point) and at Cranham; teas may be available in summer at Cooper's Hill.

Buses: Stagecoach Stroud Valleys 46 Cheltenham to Stroud via Cranham Corner, Monday to Saturday (hourly); Stagecoach Gloucester Citybus 10 Gloucester to Brockworth, daily (every 10 minutes on weekdays, half-hourly on Sundays); Stagecoach Gloucester Citybus 50 Gloucester to Cheltenham via Brockworth, Monday to Saturday (hourly).

Trains: Nearest stations are Gloucester, Cheltenham and Stroud.

Parking: There is some roadside parking close to Cranham Corner, perhaps most conveniently beside the road to Upton St Leonards at grid reference 880130. However, it would be best to leave a car in Gloucester, Cheltenham or Stroud, depending on which bus route is used.

Every county has dozens of nature reserves, of varying quality and interest, but National Nature Reserves are special. Usually known as NNRs, they protect our most important areas of wildlife habitat and are managed on behalf of the nation, mostly by English Nature, though increasingly by other approved groups such as county wildlife trusts. The Cotswold Commons and Beechwoods National Nature Reserve is one of the largest and most important areas for wildlife in Gloucestershire, comprising a mosaic of beechwoods and limestone grassland, rich in wild flowers. It includes a number of individual reserves, two of which, Buckholt Wood and Cooper's Hill Wood, are explored in this walk. Beechwoods are uncommon this

Beech trees in autumn mist. Buckholt Wood, near Cranham

far north and you would go a long way to find a finer example than Buckholt, which is managed by Gloucestershire Wildlife Trust. Although the beech is a native tree it occurs naturally only in the south, and these Gloucestershire woods mark the northern limit of its natural distribution in Britain, though, of course, it may be seen as a planted tree almost anywhere. Buckholt is an ancient woodland, as its name suggests (it's Anglo-Saxon for "beechwood"), and is mentioned in the Domesday Book. Held in common since at least the 14th century, it was traditionally used for grazing and timber production by local people. Rights of common still apply, but animals are no longer grazed as they once were.

The Walk

To begin your walk, cross to the east side of the A46 and walk down Mill Lane. Turn right at a T-junction, then left at the next, descending to cross Painswick Stream. Climb out of the valley to Mann's Court and go straight ahead on a footpath. Just before you reach a house, a waymarked post indicates a left turn which takes you behind the house, climbing to a junction where you fork left.

Fork left again as you reach the edge of Cranham and follow the path into the churchyard. Though of ancient foundation, the greater part of St James's Church was rebuilt in 1895. Fortunately, the 15th-century tower was spared, and is famous for two pairs of sheep shears carved high on the west face, probably indicating that rich wool merchants or clothiers paid for its construction. Features of interest inside the church include a fine monument to an 18th-century rector with the glorious name of Obadiah Done, who served here for 57 years.

Leave the churchyard by the lychgate and turn right along the lane to reach Cranham Common, where open limestone grassland provides a haven for increasingly rare species of wild flowers and insects. On a warm summer's day this is a great place to relax with a picnic and watch the butterflies. Fork left just by a bus stop on to a track running along the edge of the common and leading into the heart of the village.

Cranham is a small place, but it has produced at least one famous family: the Horlicks, of malted milk fame. And it used to entertain an

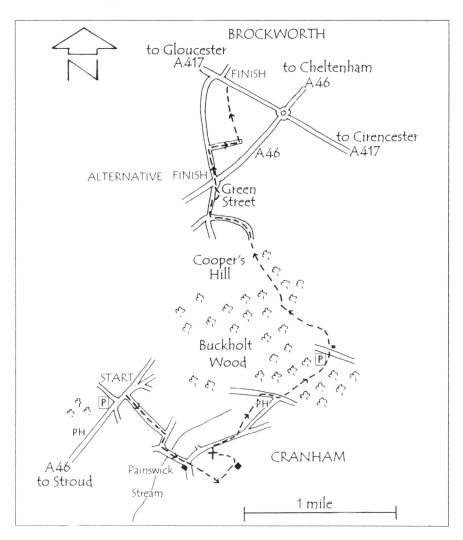

even more famous visitor, the Cheltenham-born composer Gustav Holst, who occasionally came here to play the harmonium in the church.

Go straight on past the pub then turn right when you reach a house called Brookfield. On reaching another area of grassy common, turn left on a track, pass a house called Treetops and soon fork left at a junction. A few paces further on you enter Buckholt Wood.

Though beech is the dominant tree here, a number of other species flourish, including birch, whitebeam, elder, ash, oak, holly and field maple. Unusually for a beechwood, there is a rich ground flora too, with a colourful display each spring and some uncommon species such as helleborine.

The path descends to cross a brook and climbs up again, gently. Ignore all branching paths and keep straight on to reach a parking area where a left fork takes you to a road. Cross to a footpath opposite which descends along the edge of the wood. After passing through an open gateway ignore a right fork and carry on along the main track, soon turning left to walk close to the edge of the wood on the Cotswold Way. Fork right at the next junction then go straight on at the next, still following the waymarked route.

Shortly after crossing a brook, fork left uphill into Cooper's Hill Wood. When the path emerges from the wood, continue in the same direction along a lane bordered by houses. On your left you'll soon see the near-vertical slope of Cooper's Hill (gradient of 1:2), where a cheese-rolling competition takes place every Spring Bank Holiday Monday.

This tradition goes back centuries, to medieval times or earlier. Nobody is quite sure of its original purpose, though conflicting theories abound. In its present form competitors have to launch themselves on a mad dash to catch a Double Gloucester cheese, in a wooden case, which is rolled down the slope. The cheese, which can reach speeds of 70mph, is not easily caught and minor injuries are common.

When you come to a house called Stoneleigh, a sign indicates the Cotswold Way to Painswick. Go this way if you want to complete a circular walk back to Cranham Corner. Just follow the Cotswold Way and you can't go wrong. However, this route is so well-used some may feel it is best avoided. Worse still, there are so many other waymarked footpaths and bridleways that you can hardly see the wood for the blue and yellow arrows.

For the linear walk, stay on the lane and you'll soon come to a crossroads. Turn right, descending steeply on Green Street, a narrow lane which plunges down to a hamlet of the same name. Leave the lane at a house called Green Garden and continue downhill on a track which soon rejoins the lane. Arrive at the main road, which can mark the end of the walk if you wish: there are bus stops on both sides, allowing for a return to either Stroud or Cheltenham. But time it right if you intend catching a bus here as the A46 is not a road you would want to wait beside for long. If you're intending to finish the walk at Brockworth, cross the road and continue down Green Street opposite. Then turn right on a "no through road" to Watermead, where a footpath on the left leads through a housing estate to Brockworth. There are many branching paths but if you keep straight on you'll soon come to the main road. There are bus stops either side, just a little way to the left, and buses every ten minutes or so on weekdays, half-hourly on Sundays.

Walk 2: Nailsworth and Avening

A short, easy, circular walk in delightful countryside, with an interesting village at the halfway point. Nailsworth is a small town not much visited by tourists, but with plenty of interest. There are five stiles.

Start/finish: The bus station, Old Market, Nailsworth, grid reference 849996.

Length: 5½ miles/8.8km.

Maps: OS Landranger 162, OS Pathfinder 1133.

Refreshments: Pubs, tea rooms, cafés, restaurants, take-aways and shops in Nailsworth; pubs and shop at Avening.

Buses: Stagecoach Stroud Valleys 92/93 Gloucester/Stroud to Forest Green via Nailsworth, Monday to Saturday; 29/30 Stroud to Tetbury via Nailsworth and/or Avening, Monday to Friday; 40 Stroud to Wotton-under-Edge via Nailsworth, Monday to Saturday; X26 Cheltenham to Bath via Nailsworth, Wednesdays and Saturdays.

Trains: Nearest station is Stroud.

Parking: Public car park next to the bus station in Nailsworth.

Nailsworth, a former cloth town, developed at the confluence of two steep-sided valleys, and typifies that strangely captivating meeting of industry and countryside which is the hallmark of the more developed parts of Stroud Valleys. There are plenty of former mill-workers' cottages among the charming buildings which throng its streets and alleyways and climb in tiers up the surrounding hills. There are also some grander buildings to admire, such as Stokes Croft and the Quaker Meeting House, two 17th-century buildings on Chestnut Hill; and some fine industrial buildings of the 17th, 18th and 19th centuries, such as Egypt Mill, Dunkirk Mill and Ruskin Mill, now converted to other purposes. In recent years, Nailsworth has become something of a centre for the arts, with many respected artists and craftspeople living locally and an annual arts festival each May.

Nailsworth was the last home of W.H. Davies, who lived in a cottage called Glendower in the suburb of Watledge. He was the author of *Autobiography of a Super-tramp* (1908), though he is more famous for writing the oft-quoted couplet:

> *"What is this life if, full of care,*
> *We have no time to stand and stare?"*

The Walk

If you want to start straight on the walk just cross the brook by the bus station, go through a small garden area and up steps to the parish church. If, however, you wish to see a bit of Nailsworth first, turn left (assuming you're standing at the bus station facing the brook) and walk along Old Market to a T-junction. Turn right on Spring Hill to the town centre, marked by a clock tower, then right again on Fountain Street (A46) and walk to the church.

Cross Church Street and walk along a narrow alleyway opposite the war memorial. This leads to a residential street where you turn right. At the top turn left towards open countryside, then right on to a "no through road" which is also a bridleway. It climbs gently but steadily up pastureland, with woodland on the left, and provides good retrospective views of Nailsworth and the Stroudwater Hills. On leaving the field, continue along a walled, tree-lined holloway then along the edge of a field, a tumbledown wall on your right. Over to the left you can see the little hilltop town of Minchinhampton. After passing a dilapidated stone building, go through a gate to join a track, Shipton's Grave Lane. Keep on in much the same direction along this track, with woodland on your right. After a short distance fork left to pass a barn then keep going to the right of a stone wall, ignoring all branching footpaths.

As the village of Avening comes into view ahead the bridleway forks. You should keep right on a sunken track which descends between grassy banks, rich in wild flowers in spring and early summer. On reaching a junction go to the right, still descending. At the next junction turn left to reach the main road then turn right into Avening, a former centre for the spinning and weaving industries. Once confined deep in the sheltering valley of the infant Avon, but now advancing determinedly up the steep valley sides, Avening still manages to retain some rural charm.

The church is on your right as you enter the village. Dedicated to

Church of the Holy Cross, Avening

the Holy Cross, it's a large cruciform building with an interesting story behind it. There was a Saxon church here but the present building is early Norman. Before the Conquest the manor of Avening belonged to a young man named Britric who was sent by Edward the Confessor on a diplomatic errand to the court of Baldwin, Count of Flanders. While he was there he met the Count's daughter, Matilda, who made a play for him, only to be rejected. Matilda later married William, Duke of Normandy, and so became Queen of England in 1066. Still smarting from Britric's rejection of her, she persuaded William to dispossess Britric and imprison him at Worcester, where he died. Overcome by remorse, the Queen paid for the construction of a fine new church at Avening, where masses might be said for Britric's soul. She and William stayed at Avening Court, Britric's former home, to superintend building operations. The church was consecrated on Holy Cross Day, September 14th, 1070 or 1080 (there is some uncertainty) and the Queen provided a feast for the builders, with a boar's head as the centrepiece. Today,

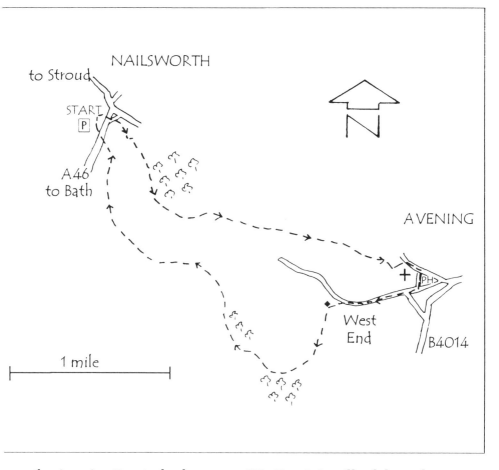

the Avening Feast, also known as "Pig Face", is still celebrated every second September. The present priest in charge of Avening is the Reverend Celia Carter, one of the first women to be ordained in the Church of England in 1994.

Return to the street and turn right, then right again by The Bell on New Inn Lane. Fork right at a junction then go straight on at the next on a "no through road" to West End. The lane gives good views down to Avening before you leave it where it crosses a brook near Orchard House. Ignore a bridleway on the left and continue ahead on a foot-path which, strictly speaking, passes through the garden of Owl

House, then over a brook into a field. However, an unofficial diversion has been provided which enables you to avoid the path through the garden if you prefer. Look for a gate on the left as you approach the house and pass through a paddock to reach the field mentioned above.

Whichever route you choose, you now turn left and follow the left-hand boundary through eight fields. Ignore a branching footpath on the left as you pass an area of woodland. The route takes you through pastureland, with woodland on your left in places. One of the fields has recently been planted with young trees. The valley through which you are walking gradually narrows as you climb almost imperceptibly between scrub-covered banks towards the head of it, after which your way continues over level ground. Soon after this you may notice a mound on your left which is a prehistoric long barrow, one of several tumuli to be found in this area.

The footpath brings you out on Shipton's Grave Lane, where you go straight on for a short distance before forking right on to Tetbury Lane. Ignore a branching footpath on the right and continue to a junction just beyond Hilltop Cottage where you fork right, still on Tetbury Lane, descending towards Nailsworth. On reaching the A46 turn right for a few paces before crossing to a narrow lane which descends into the town.

Walk 3: Whittington, Brockhampton and Sevenhampton

*A beautiful, circular walk in the tranquil upper reaches of the Coln Valley.
The terrain includes pasture, arable and woodland with gentle gradients
and good paths. There are just a few stiles, including one ladder-type.*

Start/finish: Whittington turn on A40, grid reference 013205.

Length: 6 miles/9.6km.

Maps: OS Landranger 163, OS Pathfinder 1067, OS Outdoor Leisure 45.

Refreshments: Pub in Brockhampton.

Buses: Swanbrook 53 Tewkesbury, Gloucester and Cheltenham to Oxford
via Whittington, daily; Pulham's Coaches Moreton, Stow and Bourton to
Cheltenham via Whittington, daily except winter Sundays; Perrett's Coaches
Cheltenham to Northleach via Whittington, Monday to Saturday; other less
frequent services operated mainly by Pulham's. Note that almost all buses
stop at the Whittington turn, not in the village.

Trains: Nearest station is Cheltenham.

Parking: What looks like a parking area by the A40 opposite the Whittington
turn is actually a bus stop, but there is a lay-by 300 metres to the west (grid
reference 010205).

The River Coln rises to the south-east of Cleeve Hill and flows into
the Thames at Lechlade. Its course is exquisitely beautiful in places,
making it the best loved of Cotswold rivers. Every summer that part
of its valley which contains Bibury and Arlington is submerged under a flood of tourists and their cars, a process which began over a
century ago when William Morris pronounced Bibury the most
beautiful village in England. However, there's more to the Coln Valley than Bibury and its neighbours. While those unfortunate villages
choke in a haze of petrol fumes, it's still possible to explore the upper
reaches of the Coln in peace and solitude, as this walk near the head
of the valley demonstrates.

The Walk

If you arrive by bus simply walk up the lane into Whittington, but if you arrive by car and park it in the lay-by to the west you can either walk alongside the A40 to the Whittington turn or you can take a footpath which leaves the road at the end of the lay-by, crosses a field and then turns right to Whittington. If you walk up the lane into Whittington, you'll pass 16th-century Whittington Court, and a tiny Norman church next to it, restored in 1872. Inside there are three interesting 13th- and 14th-century effigies to members of the Crupes family and a brass to Richard Cotton (died 1556) and his wife, who built Whittington Court on the site of an earlier house, of which only part of the moat survives.

Continuing up the lane into the village, a T-junction is reached by

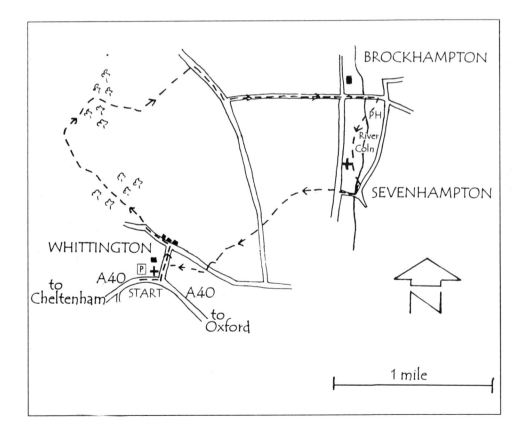

a row of attractive cottages. Turn left here and shortly fork right on a "no through road" which becomes a bridleway. Though it leads through woodland it also allows glimpses of old quarry workings, now grassed over and providing ideal conditions for a range of limestone-loving flowers.

On leaving the wood the bridleway skirts more disused quarries then contours round the base of a twin-domed hill before passing more woodland to reach a T-junction. Turn right through Puckham Wood, and on emerging from the trees continue to a junction with a footpath. Bear left, following an obvious track over the hill. This leads to an unfenced lane where you turn right, then first left along Park Lane. The view from here is splendid as you have been steadily climbing, probably without realising it, to a height of 890ft. (272 metres).

As you approach a crossroads the imposing mansion of Brockhampton Park comes into view. Built in 1639, but much altered in the 19th century, it now presents a Victorian "Tudor" face to the world. It was for many years the home of the Craven family, associated with Craven Arms in Shropshire, but it has now been divided into flats. George III is said to have dined here in 1788 on the occasion of his visit to Cheltenham. The estate once included a deer park, famous for a herd of white deer.

Go straight on into Brockhampton village, crossing the infant Coln on the way. It's only a tiny village, but there are some lovely cottages to admire before you turn right along a "no through road" to a pub, the Craven Arms. Next to it, what looks like a farmhouse, apart from its red-brick chimney, proves to be the Old Brewery, in operation until the 1930s. Across the way is a cottage with an unusual sundial.

A signpost indicates a footpath to Sevenhampton. Overgrown at first, it soon improves and is fully waymarked, heading south along the valley to emerge in the churchyard at Sevenhampton, bright with flowers and endowed with some characteristic Cotswold table tombs. St Andrew's Church is of Norman origin but was extended by a bequest of John Camber, a wealthy wool merchant, who died in 1497. It must be the smallest wool church in the Cotswolds. Nearby

The Coln Valley between Brockhampton and Sevenhampton.

stands Sevenhampton Manor, an elegant, 16th-century building partially destroyed by fire in the 1950s.

Leave the churchyard by the main gate, joining a footpath opposite which leads to Lower Sevenhampton. Here you cross the Coln and continue beside it to join a lane. This is a particularly lovely spot, with the old cottages seeming to grow out of the lush vegetation fringing the river.

Sevenhampton is often claimed to be relatively recent, as villages go, developing only in the Middle Ages after another village, Sennington, a little to the west, had been abandoned, possibly because of the Black Death. Given that Sevenhampton's church is of Norman origin, this is an unlikely claim. The two must always have been separate villages, despite what some see as the similarity of their names. Sennington was not unusual in being abandoned; many other villages in the area suffered the same fate.

Cross the Coln by a footbridge next to a ford and walk up the lane to a road. Join a footpath opposite which goes straight ahead along field edges. When you reach a damaged section in the wall on your right, it's time to bear left across two fields to a lane. There are two footpaths opposite. Take the left-hand one, going diagonally across two fields then down the right-hand edge of another before turning left to a lane. Cross to a footpath opposite and follow this around the right-hand edge of a field to reach another. The path goes more or less straight across to reach the lane near Whittington Court. On the way across this final field you'll notice a number of humps and holloways, highlighted by a strong growth of nettles. This is the site of the original village of Whittington, deserted, like Sennington, some time in the Middle Ages. The site of a Roman villa has also been discovered in the same field.

Walk 4: Northleach and Yanworth

A short circular walk which includes one steep but very brief slope, and uses field paths, tracks and quiet lanes, with just eight stiles. The terrain is a mixture of arable and pasture. Highlights include one of the finest churches in England and one of the most unspoilt villages in the Cotswolds.

Start/finish: The Market Place, Northleach, grid reference 114146.

Length: 6 miles/9.6km.

Maps: OS Landranger 163, OS Pathfinder 1090, OS Outdoor Leisure 45.

Refreshments: Pubs, tea rooms, restaurant and shops in Northleach.

Buses: Swanbrook 53 Tewkesbury, Gloucester and Cheltenham to Oxford via Northleach, daily; Perrett's Coaches Cheltenham to Northleach, Monday to Saturday. Other infrequent services, provided by Pulham's, Ebley and Thamesdown, operate from Cheltenham, Cirencester and Stow.

Coaches: National Express 347 Taunton and/or Bristol to Cambridge and/or Great Yarmouth via Northleach, daily.

Trains: Nearest station is Cheltenham.

Parking: Northleach.

The area centred on Northleach is rolling wold country divided by drystone walls and would probably typify the popular conception of what constitutes the Cotswolds if it were not that sheep have mainly given way to cereals. It's still attractive enough, however, and is greatly enhanced by the fact that two of Cotswold's loveliest rivers, the Coln and the Leach, have carved gentle valleys into the wolds. There are two types of village here; those that have snuggled into sheltered locations in the valleys, and those that have rooted defiantly into the rather bleaker soil of the high wold. It is the latter type that is encountered in this walk in the form of remote, exposed and unspoilt Yanworth.

The town of Northleach, however, does occupy the valley, sitting on the north bank of the River Leach, with the Roman Fosse Way running past its west end. The Gloucester to London road used to pass right through it, but now bypasses it to the north, leaving the

Yanworth church

old road as Northleach's High Street. This position on major lines of communication was just one of the factors which helped Northleach to prosper in the past, it was also one of the most important wool towns, third only to Chipping Campden and Cirencester.

It was granted its market charter in 1220 by Henry III and it is likely that the market was held in the area now known as The Green as well as in what is still called Market Place, though there is no longer a market. Both Market Place and The Green have been given over to car parking, quite spoiling what would otherwise be an extremely attractive town centre. The High Street boasts over 70 properties of historic and/or architectural interest, some of them, unusually for Cotswold, half-timbered, though the overall impression, especially if you approach from the west, is of unbroken harmony in stone, with almost nothing, except the cars, out of place.

As well as looking round the tiny town centre, it's well worth investigating the side streets and alleyways, which have their origins in the medieval period – street names such as Antelope Lane, Guggle Lane, The Peep and All Alone just beg to be explored.

Northleach's greatest prosperity was from 1340 to 1540 when Cotswold wool was in great demand in Europe and the small town became an important international market for the buying and export of raw wool. The merchants who grew rich on this trade poured some of their wealth back into the town, most obviously in the magnificent form of the church of St Peter and St Paul, which is sometimes known as the "Cathedral of the Cotswolds". The oldest part of the present building is the tower, which dates from about 1350, but most of it is 15th-century work in the Perpendicular style. The exterior is beautiful and enormously impressive, with the south porch often considered the finest in the country. However, some may find the interior rather stark, though it does contain a remarkable collection of memorial brasses, most of which depict wool merchants standing over sheep and woolsacks. Incidentally, people have been known to walk around searching for the brasses and leave in frustration without finding them – look on the floor, not the walls.

The Walk

To begin your walk, pass through the churchyard to leave it at the far right corner. Entering a field, turn left and walk beside a wall which encloses a cemetery. When you reach the corner of the cemetery head for the bottom right corner of the field. Keep on in the same direction over another field, crossing the little River Leach at a footbridge and turning right along a narrow, hummocky field, climbing gently to its top left corner. A number of springs rise in the field and feed into a pool on your right. This is one of several places in Gloucestershire known as Seven Springs and is said by some to be the source of the River Leach, which others say rises in Hampnett.

Turn right along a lane and keep straight on, soon crossing the Fosse Way (A429). Keep straight on again at a crossroads but only for a few paces, to where two stone stiles give access to a footpath on the right. Walk across a field, aiming to the left of a pylon then for a gap in a wall. Cross a second field and go through a gate into a third, joining the Monarch's Way. Go straight on along the edge of the field as Yanworth comes into view ahead; a grey cluster of hilltop buildings set against the shaggy backdrop of Chedworth Woods.

The track descends towards Oxpens Farm. Turn right past the

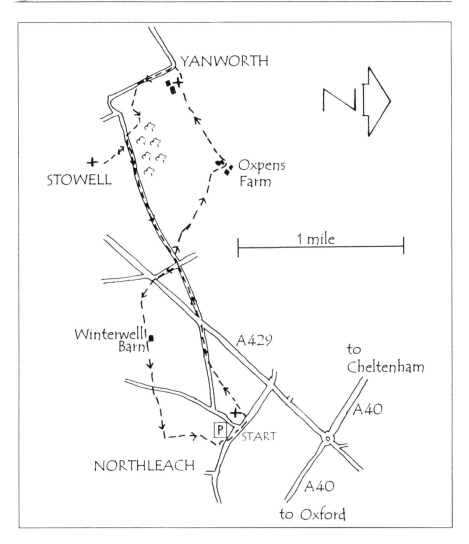

farmhouse then take the first left, passing between barns, to a junction where you turn right. Follow the track round to the left as it leaves the farm and heads towards Yanworth. When it bends sharp right, the right of way, strictly speaking, actually goes straight on over a field, cutting the corner to rejoin the track by a brook.

The track now climbs to Yanworth, a typical high wold village of solid, substantial farm buildings standing four-square against the wind. A gate gives access to the churchyard and a small, endearingly odd-looking, 12th-century church. Inside there are intriguing carved heads and a 16th-century wall painting of Time, or Death, depicted as a skeleton with a scythe, a shroud and a sexton's shovel. On the exterior south wall a beautifully inscribed brass plate in memory of Elizabeth Bicknell features a skull and crossbones. Across the way is Church Farm, comprising a long, low farmhouse and a superb range of sturdy outbuildings, in complete harmony with their setting.

Leaving the churchyard by the main gate, turn right up the lane to reach a junction with the Macmillan Way. Turn left to another junction on the edge of the village. Our route now is to the left, down into the valley, but it's worth a look at Yanworth first for it's an unusually unspoilt village, with few jarring notes other than the occasional suburban conifer and a sad clutter of overhead power lines.

Resuming the walk, head downhill from Yanworth until, soon after passing a turning for the church, you come to a point where there are footpaths either side of the lane. Join the one on the left, which descends to cross a stream then climbs straight up a steep slope through a belt of woodland. At the top turn left and follow the path round to the lane. Turn left, soon reaching the drive to Stowell. Despite the "private" sign displayed here you can walk along the drive to visit Stowell Church if you wish. This small, Norman building has been much altered but is remarkable for the survival of a Doom painting (a representation of Judgement Day) created between 1150 and 1200. It's one of the most precious works of its kind still surviving. Opposite the church is an imposing Jacobean house, Stowell Park, set in a walled garden on top of a slope with fine views of the Coln Valley.

Return along the drive to the lane and turn right between high, grassy banks overflowing with limestone-loving wild flowers in spring and early summer. At a crossroads turn right then shortly cross the Fosse Way and go straight on along a footpath opposite which follows an unmistakable course, passing Winterwell Barn, to another lane.

Cross over and continue on the footpath until another one crosses it. Turn left here along the edge of a field, enjoying good views of the church at Northleach. Go over a stile in the field corner and bear slightly to the right as you descend the next field towards a children's play area. Go through a kissing gate to join a footpath into town.

Walk 5: Winchcombe and Sudeley

A short circular walk which includes a steady climb to the top of a ridge, offering excellent views. The return leg is all downhill, the paths are easy to follow and there are only a few stiles. Winchcombe is a lovely town, well worth exploration either before or after your walk.

Start/finish: Abbey Terrace, Winchcombe, grid reference 024282.

Length: 6½ miles/10.5km.

Maps: OS Landranger 163, OS Pathfinder 1067, OS Outdoor Leisure 45.

Refreshments: Pubs, tea rooms, restaurants, take-aways and shops in Winchcombe.

Buses: Castleways Coaches 606 Willersey to Cheltenham via Winchcombe, Monday to Saturday; Marchant's Coaches Cheltenham to Winchcombe, evenings and Sundays. Other less frequent services are operated by Barry's, Castleways, Cresswell's and Stagecoach Stroud Valleys.

Trains: Nearest station is Cheltenham.

Parking: Public car parks in Winchcombe.

Winchcombe is a fine example of a small Cotswold town fitting perfectly into its surroundings. The houses, built of local stone, nestle in the lovely valley of the River Isbourne, overlooked by Salters Hill, Langley Hill, Sudeley Hill and historic Sudeley Castle. The town has an illustrious past, having been, in the Saxon period, the most important Cotswold town and a provincial capital of the kingdom of Mercia, controlling the northern approaches to the wolds. In the early 11th century it was briefly the capital of Wincelcumbeshire, before this long-vanished county was absorbed into Gloucestershire.

Long before this, however, Winchcombe had been established as a regional capital by King Offa, who also founded a nunnery there in 788. His son Kenulf established an abbey on the same site in 798 but it suffered many vicissitudes, being burned down and rebuilt on at least two occasions before the Dissolution of the Monasteries, when its destruction was entrusted to Lord Thomas Seymour of Sudeley, a task he fulfilled so thoroughly that almost no trace remains today.

The abbey had been the site of a shrine to Kenulf's son Kenelm, Prince of Mercia, murdered in 819 at the age of seven on the orders of his envious sister Quendrida. Kenelm died at Romsley in Worcestershire, but his body was taken back to Winchcombe and his story (probably invented by the monks of Winchcombe) was told by several chroniclers with many variations, but perhaps most famously by William of Malmesbury in the early 12th century.

Thousands of pilgrims came to visit not only Kenelm's shrine at Winchcombe Abbey, but also nearby Hailes Abbey, which boasted a phial of Christ's blood (exposed at the Dissolution as a mixture of honey and saffron). This brought enormous prosperity to Winchcombe, which also held weekly markets and a number of annual fairs. The timber-framed George Inn, built during the reign of Henry VII by Abbot Richard Kidderminster, whose initials are carved on the spandrels of the doorway, was one of several where the pilgrims stayed. The 15th-century parish church, dedicated to St Peter, is a good example of the later Perpendicular style, with its battlemented tower adorned with pinnacles and crockets. It is famous for its collection of 40 or so grotesque gargoyles, sometimes called the Winchcombe Worthies and said to have been based on prominent townsfolk. The spacious interior contains an altar cloth reputedly embroidered by Catherine of Aragon, one of three of Henry VIII's wives to be associated with Winchcombe. The others are Anne Boleyn, who visited Sudeley Castle on a hunting expedition with the king in 1532, and Catherine Parr, who lived at Sudeley after Henry's death with her fourth husband, Sir Thomas Seymour. Catherine is buried in the castle chapel.

Sudeley Castle, now the home of Lord and Lady Ashcombe, is set in extensive formal gardens on the edge of Winchcombe and open to the public daily from April to October (01242 602308). Its origins and royal connections go back to the 10th century, though the oldest parts of the present building were erected in the 15th century. Sudeley suffered badly in the Civil War and lay in ruins for 200 years until purchased by the Dent brothers of Worcester in the 1830s. Their sympathetic restoration resulted in the splendid buildings we see today.

Sudeley attracts plenty of visitors but, thankfully, Winchcombe,

Sudeley Castle, Winchcombe

despite its charms, has resisted the temptation to sell out to tourism and remains a delightful place, though with the usual traffic problems. It's popular with walkers as a number of waymarked paths meet here – the Cotswold Way, Gloucestershire Way, Wardens' Way, Windrush Way and Wychavon Way. The Cotswold Way enters Winchcombe from the north on Puck Pit Lane, the ancient pilgrims' route to Hailes Abbey.

The Walk

This walk incorporates parts of the Wardens' Way and Windrush Way, two routes linking Winchcombe with Bourton-on-the-Water by contrasting routes. Leave Winchcombe on the Wardens' Way, which goes along picturesque Vineyard Street towards Sudeley Castle. When you reach a cattle grid enter a field and keep close to the fence until it turns a corner, then keep straight on to a dead tree before aiming for a tall poplar in the left corner. You'll find a stile nearby and from now on detailed directions are superfluous because the Wardens' Way is clearly waymarked, using a green "W" on the familiar yellow arrow.

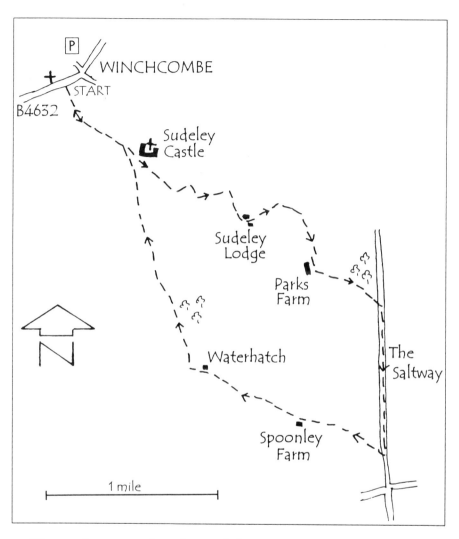

The path passes close by Sudeley Castle before beginning the climb up Sudeley Hill. When you pass Sudeley Lodge, have a look at the plaque which records a visit by George III in 1788 while the king was staying at Cheltenham to bestow royal approval on what was becoming an increasingly fashionable spa. While he was there he seems to have spent a fair amount of time exploring the countryside for a number of places claim a connection.

A further half mile or so and you come to Parks Farm – don't miss the left turn here. Before long you'll reach an unclassified ridge-top road, once a packhorse route for the transport of salt from Droitwich in Worcestershire to Lechlade on the Thames, and still known as the Salt Way. This does not mean that it was developed by the salt traders, who simply used prehistoric routes already in existence. Most of these tended to be along ridges where early man had found the going was easier, avoiding the tangled forests, treacherous marshes and wild animals of the valleys.

Turn right and follow the Salt Way for nearly a mile until you come to a footpath on the right, part of the Windrush Way. Join this and follow the surfaced track which descends past Spoonley Farm, with the remains of a Roman villa excavated in the 19th century hidden in Spoonley Wood a little to the north, and walk down Cole's Hill to Waterhatch. The path then runs on through the pleasant valley of Beesmoor Brook, a tributary of the River Isbourne, to rejoin your outward route near Sudeley Castle.

Walk 6: Moreton-in-Marsh to Chipping Campden

Well-defined footpaths, mostly across pastureland, with just two gentle slopes and nine stiles. Chipping Campden has frequently been described as the loveliest small town in England, which is more than enough to make it a worthwhile objective of this beautiful linear walk via Blockley.

Start: Moreton-in-Marsh Station, grid reference 206327.

Finish: The High Street, Chipping Campden, grid reference 151392.

Length: 7 miles/11.2km.

Maps: OS Landranger 151, OS Pathfinders 1043 and 1044, OS Outdoor Leisure 45.

Refreshments: Pubs, tea rooms, restaurants, take-aways and shops in Moreton and Campden; pubs, tea room and shop in Blockley; pub at Broad Campden.

Buses: Castleways Coaches 569 "Cotswold Explorer" Evesham to Moreton via Blockley and Chipping Campden, daily except winter Sundays; Stagecoach Midland Red 21 "Cotswold Shuttle" Stratford to Bourton via Moreton, daily; 22 Stratford to Broadway via Chipping Campden, Monday to Saturday; Pulham's Coaches Cheltenham, Bourton and Stow to Moreton, daily except winter Sundays. Other less frequent services, provided by Baker's, Barry's, Castleways, Cresswell's, Jeff's, Pulham's, Stagecoach, Thamesdown and Villager operate to Moreton from all over Gloucestershire and from towns beyond the county, such as Banbury, Charlbury, Evesham, Pershore, Shipston, Stratford, Swindon, Witney and Woodstock, though several of them run only on Tuesdays.

Coaches: National Express 511 Great Malvern to London via Moreton, daily.

Trains: Thames Trains and Great Western operate daily services to Moreton on the Cotswold Line.

Parking: Public car park next to the railway station.

Moreton-in-Marsh straddles the Fosse Way in the fertile Vale of Evenlode and also lies astride the main road from London and Oxford to Worcester and Mid Wales. Like most Cotswold towns, Moreton prospered as a centre for the wool and cloth trades but was never pre-eminent in these and they had more or less died out by the Stuart era. In 1742 a linen trade was established. This, too, failed to flourish indefinitely, but Moreton became an important coaching town and the coming of the railway in 1853 proved of further benefit once the town had recovered from the subsequent decline in coaching. For more information about Moreton turn to Walk 15.

The Walk

Join Corders Lane, close to the Victorian town hall in the middle of the High Street. At a junction go straight ahead on a footpath which follows a well-trodden, waymarked route across lush buttercup meadows. After 1½ miles there is a choice of footpaths. Keep straight on, joining the Heart of England Way and following it past Batsford Park, a large mansion in Victorian "Tudor" style (1888-92) which is famous for its arboretum. The grounds were landscaped in the 1880s by Bertie Mitford, the first Lord Redesdale, and an ancestor of the six famous Mitford sisters. He had entered diplomatic service in Japan around 1850 and was much influenced by oriental ideas, hence the bronze Buddha which adorns the arboretum. Batsford is one of the largest privately-owned collections of trees in Britain and is open daily to the public from March to November (01608 650722).

The path now climbs uphill past plantations to a lane on top of a ridge. Cross the lane and go straight on, descending to meet a walled, tree-lined track. The Heart of England Way turns left for a direct descent into Blockley, but for a more interesting route turn right instead. Before long, you may notice that a bridleway runs alongside the footpath, on the other side of the wall on your left. This bridleway leads down to Blockley but there is no means of joining it until the green lane comes to an end, at which point you can turn left onto the bridleway and follow it to Blockley.

Reaching the village, turn right, then left uphill to the church, a late Norman building dedicated to St Peter and St Paul, with a fine Gothic tower which was rebuilt in 1725 after storm damage. The churchyard contains a number of 18th-century table tombs.

Emerge from the top end of the churchyard on to Bell Lane. Your onward route is straight ahead up Bell Bank, rejoining the Heart of England Way. First, however, it's well worth stopping to explore the village, which is beautifully situated, its steep streets full of character.

The manor of Blockley was bought from King Burgred of Mercia by the Bishop of Worcester in 855 and successive bishops kept up to 2000 sheep on Blockley's pastures, selling the wool to Chipping Campden merchants. In 1086 Domesday Book recorded Blockley as the second largest settlement in Worcestershire, with 12 mills (Blockley was not transferred to Gloucestershire until 1931). Several mill ponds survive, as do the mill workers' cottages. Blockley was well-placed to become an early industrial village, thanks to Blockley Brook, which for centuries drove the mills. As early as the 12th century water power was grinding corn and fulling woollen cloth, and by the 19th century there were also mills for silk, cider, threshing and paper.

The hamlet of Broad Campden, on the edge of Chipping Campden

As many as eight silk mills once flourished, employing 800 people and supplying silk to the Coventry ribbon manufacturers. Silk throwsting (cleansing) was introduced in the late 17th century by James Rushout, the son of a Flemish immigrant. Both the trade and the Rushouts flourished, with a later Rushout becoming the first Lord Northwick. The family lived at Northwick Park, built in 1686, which was later the home of the Spencer-Churchills. The house has since been partly subdivided into apartments. The silk trade was killed by foreign competition and by 1885 the mills had been converted to other uses. In 1887 one of them was used to generate electricity and Blockley claims to be the first English village to have been lit by electricity.

Returning to Bell Bank, walk uphill then turn right at a junction. At the next one join a footpath opposite and cross two fields before bearing right down a slope. Cross a brook and bear right uphill. After passing through a gate turn right to a gap in the hedge and join a lane, leaving the Heart of England Way and turning left.

After about half a mile, join a footpath on the right, descending on a track until a stile on the left gives access to woodland bordering the lane. Walk through the trees until a path on the left allows you to rejoin the lane and cross to another footpath opposite. After admiring the view of Chipping Campden descend a slope then go straight on to reach the green in the centre of the lovely hamlet of Broad Campden, quietly tucked away in a small valley. Among the attractive buildings here are an 18th-century Quaker meeting house and a house converted in the early years of this century from a derelict Norman chapel by C.R. Ashbee, a follower of William Morris and founder of the Chipping Campden Guild of Handicrafts.

Rejoin the Heart of England Way and follow it to Chipping Campden. As you approach the town join George Lane, which leads to the Noel Arms and the High Street. If you are catching a bus to Evesham your stop is directly opposite, next to the stone which marks the beginning of the Cotswold Way. If you're returning to Moreton, either for the train or to retrieve your car, turn left for a few yards to the bus stop by the library.

First, however, you will surely want to explore this most beautiful of all Cotswold market towns, with its long, gracefully curving High Street described by H.J. Massingham as "the most beautiful street in Europe". But Massingham was writing in 1937 when cars were still uncommon. If traffic were to be banned from the High Street the truth of his words would be fully apparent once more.

Chipping Campden has a long history: there was a weekly market here as early as 1180 ("Chipping" is from a Saxon word for market) and three annual fairs by 1247. It was at the height of its prosperity in the later Middle Ages when Cotswold wool was famous throughout Western Europe, and the most prominent merchants achieved a kind of immortality – William Grevel, for instance, who built Grevel House in about 1380. On his memorial in the church Grevel is de-

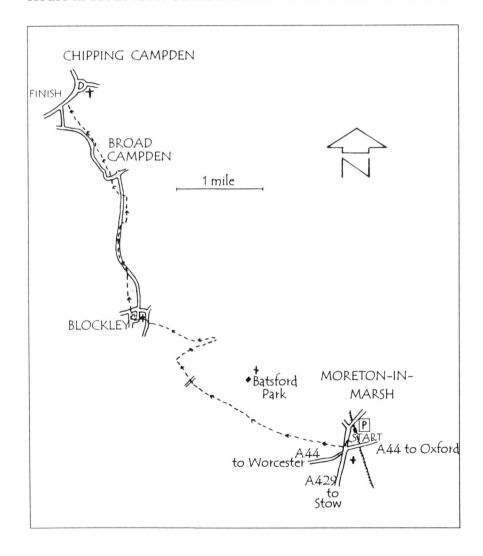

scribed as "the flower of the wool merchants of all England". He contributed much to the beauty of Campden, leaving large sums of money on his death in 1401 for restoration of the church. Grevel is thought to be the model for the merchant in Chaucer's *Canterbury Tales*.

Over 600 years on, Grevel House is still there and still magnificent, but it is not the oldest building in the High Street; that honour goes to the Woolstaplers' Hall of 1340. But more famous than either is the gabled, open-bayed Market Hall, built in 1627 by Sir Baptist Hicks, who bought the manor of Campden in the time of James I. Hicks was the son of a Gloucestershire merchant who set up business in London. He became enormously rich, even lending money to the king. Created Viscount Campden in 1629, he was responsible for the lovely almshouses near the church (1612) and Campden House, an Italian-style mansion which once occupied a glorious setting nearby. All but a few remnants was destroyed by fire in 1645, set deliberately by a Royalist commander to prevent it falling into enemy hands.

The Norman church is the most celebrated structure of all, wool merchants' money having transformed it in the 15th century into one of the most sublime examples of the builder's art, its superb tower exemplifying the appeal of Perpendicular architecture. Work began about 1450 and took 50 years to complete but it has a great consistency of style and workmanship.

The well-preserved appearance of Chipping Campden owes much to the Campden Trust, established by architects and craftsmen in 1929. The Trust has restored numerous properties and helped ensure that the High Street is not marred by hideous modern shop fronts or obtrusive power lines. Now, if they could just find a way of getting rid of the traffic...

Walk 7: Broadway, Buckland and Stanton

An undulating, but not overly strenuous, circular walk in glorious countryside, visiting one of the loveliest of all Cotswold villages, secluded little Stanton, tucked away in a sheltered combe below the scarp. The paths are good but there are two dozen stiles to clamber over.

Start/finish: The High Street, Broadway, grid reference 095375.

Length: 7 miles/11.2km.

Maps: OS Landranger 150, OS Pathfinder 1043, OS Outdoor Leisure 45.

Refreshments: Pubs, tea rooms, restaurants and shops in Broadway (but not all of them welcome dogs, children or muddy boots); pub at Stanton.

Buses: Castleways Coaches 569 "Cotswold Explorer" Evesham to Moreton via Broadway, daily except winter Sundays; Castleways/Springs' 559 Willersey to Evesham via Broadway, Monday to Saturday; Castleways 606 Willersey to Cheltenham via Broadway, Monday to Saturday; Stagecoach Midland Red 21 "Cotswold Shuttle" Stratford to Bourton via Broadway, daily; 22 Stratford to Broadway, Monday to Saturday. Other less frequent services also operate, provided by Barry's, Castleways, Cresswell's, Pulham's, Springs' and Stagecoach Stroud Valleys.

Coaches: National Express 511 Great Malvern to London via Broadway, daily.

Trains: Nearest station is Evesham.

Parking: Public car parks in Broadway.

Broadway looks so thoroughly "Cotswold" that many visitors assume it's in Gloucestershire, but the parish is actually a peninsular of Worcestershire intruding into its neighbour. More than one commentator has declared Broadway "the most beautiful village in England", with the result that it is now an over-priced honeypot attracting throngs of traffic and tourists. Upmarket boutiques, gift shops and even a mini shopping mall are some of the indignities which have been inflicted on what was once an agricultural village. Nonetheless, it is undeniably beautiful, its main street rising towards the wooded slopes of Fish Hill so that there is almost nowhere in the village from where trees and hill pasture are not visible. Gracious buildings of golden stone spanning seven centuries line the High Street, and from their garden walls wisteria, clematis and old-fashioned roses spill over towards the grass verges which culminate in a green at the western end of the village. Such beauty still transcends the tourist tat, especially out of season, when early morning or evening sun makes the mellow stone glow with warmth and life.

Broadway's buildings come in a variety of styles, but the blend is one of deep harmony thanks to the unifying effect of the stone. The oldest houses in town are ecclesiastical in origin, with Abbot's Grange built as a summer palace for the Abbot of Evesham, and Prior's Manse constructed for the Prior of Worcester. Both date from about 1320. One of the finest buildings is the world-famous Lygon Arms, where both Charles I and Cromwell are said to have stayed, though presumably not on the same night. Though it bears the date 1620, there has been a hotel on this site since at least 1532, when it was known as the White Hart. The new name commemorates local landowner General Lygon, who had his estate planted with clumps of trees in the same formation as the troops at the battle of Waterloo.

Broadway was largely an agricultural village for many centuries, but its position on or close to a number of ancient roads meant it also had a tradition of catering for travellers. In the 18th century it benefited from the development of turnpikes, becoming an important staging post on the London to Worcester road. At the height of the coaching era it had between 20 and 30 inns to cater for travellers. The coming of the railway in 1856 spelt the end for coaches, but after an initial decline in Broadway's fortunes the new railway began to bring in tourists and the village became a fashionable centre for writers, artists and craftsmen, including the influential William Morris.

Many visitors seem content to just mill around the green and the western end of the High Street, probably because this is where the shops are, but those who walk up towards the east end are rewarded with some of Broadway's most charming houses, nearly all of which were built as farmhouses or farm workers' cottages in the 17th and 18th centuries. The Cotswold Way leads up from this part of the High Street to Broadway Tower, well worth a visit, even if just for the spectacular view.

Broadway Tower

The Walk

The walk described here, however, heads not for the tower, but for two villages, Buckland and Stanton, which epitomise all that is special about Cotswold. Begin at the green at the western end of the High Street and turn left on Church Street, also known as Snowshill Road. Soon after passing St Michael's Church, a rather ugly building of 1839, join the Cotswold Way on the right and follow it across two fields to West End Lane. Cross over, leaving the Cotswold Way and joining a footpath to Buckland.

Walk up a slope to enter woodland and at a fork keep right, close to the edge of the wood. Fork right again at another junction, enjoying good views of the Vale of Evesham and Bredon Hill. Leaving the wood, enter a field and go across Burhill to a path junction where you fork right to reach Buckland, snugly situated in a combe below the hill.

As you enter the village you pass The Old Rectory, which dates from the 14th century and was extended by the Rector William Grafton some time between 1466 and 1480. It contains a stained-glass window from that time which depicts the arms of Edward IV.

Turn left on the main street, passing more attractive houses before you reach 12th-century St Michael's Church, one of the most interesting in Gloucestershire. It's full of treasures, including outstanding wooden furnishings, some 15th-century glass restored by William Morris, and the 16th-century Buckland bowl, in maplewood and silver, once used as a loving cup at village weddings. Best of all are the 15th-century roof timbers painted with roses and strange triangular faces.

Continue along the street to find a path on the right by The Mill Close. Entering a field, turn right and follow a clear path. When you enter a large field, with scrub and woodland on the left and a view of Laverton ahead, turn left, passing through the woodland to enter pasture. Just keep on in much the same direction, contouring around the side of the hill, towards Stanton. As you approach more closely, keep left to join a track then descend to the village. Stanton has a wonderful situation and is crammed with gorgeous houses, most of which were built between 1570 and 1650, a period known as "The Great Rebuilding" by landscape historians, when the prosper-

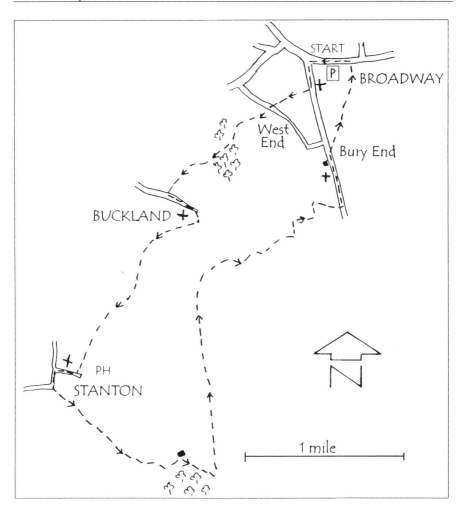

ity of yeoman farmers enabled them to build substantial houses. Those at Stanton were sensitively restored by a discerning and benevolent squire, Sir Philip Stott, an architect who bought the rather decayed manor of Stanton in 1906.

John Wesley, who often stayed with friends in Stanton, preached several sermons at the late Norman church, dedicated to St Michael and All Angels, which has a 15th-century tower topped with a slender spire and a lovely, two-storey, Perpendicular porch, much bepinnacled and battlemented.

Turn right through the village, then left at a junction, passing The Manor, with the date 1577 carved above the door and the initials TW for its builder, Thomas Warren of Snowshill. At the drive to Chestnut Farm, join a bridleway signed to Shenbarrow, Snowshill and Stanway. This is also the route of the Cotswold Way, but when the latter makes a right turn don't follow it, keep straight on along the bridleway instead. It climbs steadily uphill to reach Shenbarrow Buildings and a junction where you turn right. Turn left at the next then go straight on to a T-junction to turn left on a track.

When the Cotswold Way crosses the track, fork right to join it, following it as far as a junction by a barn where you leave it. There are two footpaths on the right; take the right-hand one, a fenced path which follows the edge of woodland then zigzags its way down fields to a road where you turn left.

Pass St Eadburga's Church and The Court House, a beautiful building with an idiosyncratic display of topiary yews dominating its garden. This was once the manor house but only the gateway of the original building survives. The cruciform church contains examples of Norman, Early English, Decorated and Perpendicular architecture and has an unspoilt, atmospheric interior.

This area is known as Bury End and predates Broadway, but the monks of Pershore Abbey established a market at what, even in 1251, was the junction of several roads, and Broadway grew up on its present site while Bury End was left to stagnate. Its situation is quiet and remote from the village, and this made it all the easier for a gang of body-snatchers, led by the parson's son, to operate at the beginning of the 19th century. There was a brisk, though obviously illegal, trade at this period in bodies for dissection. Medical schools would pay up to £20 for a corpse in good condition, before decomposition had set in. Here at Bury End the bodies were often left in a cattle byre while awaiting sale but in 1831 a decomposing corpse was dumped in the manure heap by the byre. A week later it was discovered and the so-called Resurrectionists brought to justice.

Soon after passing the church join a footpath on the right which follows a well-trodden route across fields to Broadway. This path is the one by which villagers made their way to church for centuries and in an Enclosure Award of 1771 it was named as "the ancient Churchway" with a specified width of 4 feet, ensuring it was wide enough for a corpse to be carried for burial.

Walk 8: Dursley to Nailsworth

A rewarding linear walk which avoids the obvious destinations around Dursley (Cam Peak, Nibley Knoll etc.) in favour of the lovely beechwoods which fringe the town. Once the woods are left behind, pasture and arable fields lead via Uley and Owlpen to the interesting little town of Nailsworth. There are a few short, steep climbs but it is an easy walk on the whole, with just eight stiles.

Start: Market Place, Dursley, grid reference 757982.

Finish: Old Market, Nailsworth, grid reference 849997.

Length: 8 miles/12.9km.

Maps: OS Landranger 162, OS Pathfinders 1132 and 1133.

Refreshments: Pubs, tea rooms, cafés, restaurants, take-aways and shops in Dursley and Nailsworth; pub, tea room and shop in Uley; restaurant (seasonal) at Owlpen.

Buses: Stagecoach Stroud Valleys 16 from Stroud and Stonehouse to Uley via Dursley, Monday to Saturday; 30 from Stroud to Tetbury via Nailsworth, Monday to Friday; 40 from Stroud to Wotton-under-Edge via Nailsworth, Monday to Saturday; 91 Gloucester to Dursley, daily; 92/93 Gloucester to Forest Green via Stroud and Nailsworth, Monday to Saturday; Badgerline 309 Bristol to Dursley, Monday to Saturday.

Trains: Nearest station is Cam and Dursley (3 miles/4.8km) and a bus link is provided. However, stations at Stroud, Stonehouse or Gloucester are more convenient for this walk.

Parking: Public car parks in Stroud, Stonehouse or Gloucester (there is little point in leaving a car at Dursley as there is no direct bus route between Dursley and Nailsworth).

Dursley is a busy little market town sheltered by steep, beech-rimmed slopes. Though the Cotswold Way passes through the town, it's not an obvious tourist destination and doesn't make it into all the guide books. Yet the beechwoods which overlook it are just one aspect of the superb countryside from which it benefits. As far as its situation is concerned, Dursley could hardly be improved upon. It sits below a substantial spur which juts out from the main Cotswold escarpment and culminates in Stinchcombe Hill, a notable view-point and the most westerly point in the Cotswolds.

Dursley is worth exploring before you leave, though little re-mains of the medieval town which was granted its market charter in 1471 by Edward IV. There are, however, some fine 18th-century houses in Long Street and Market Place, while the open-bayed, arched and gabled Market House, with its recessed statue of Queen Anne, is still the focal point of the town, as it has been since its con-struction in 1738. Dursley was a centre of the cloth trade between the 15th and 18th centuries, but in time competition from the Penni-nes drove the Cotswold mills out of business and Dursley moved into engineering instead.

The Walk

With the Market House and the church on your left, walk down Sil-ver Street then straight on along Bull Pitch before turning right on to Woodmancote. A little further on turn right on to Fort Lane and at the top of it fork left, soon entering Hermitage Wood, one of the beechwoods which add such distinction to Dursley's setting.

Turn left along the lower edge of the wood to reach a major junc-tion at the top of Nunnery Lane. Turn right on to a bridleway and fol-low it to the top of the hill then turn left along a lane. There is a multitude of confusing paths within the wood on your left, but the idea is to join a bridleway running parallel with the lane, just inside the wood. If you keep close to the woodland edge you can't go far wrong.

The bridleway soon becomes clearer and then bears away from the woodland edge to meet a footpath, which branches left and is waymarked with yellow arrows. Join the footpath, which descends steeply to a lane that you cross to rejoin the footpath as it resumes, al-most opposite. It runs along the lower edge of more woodland (Durs-ley Wood, Folly Wood and Coopers Wood) and you should resist the temptation to take any of the paths which branch right. Eventually the path leaves the wood by way of a mossy, ferny holloway over-hung with holly and beech, which descends to join a lane. Turn right through the tiny communities of Elcombe and Shadwell. The two

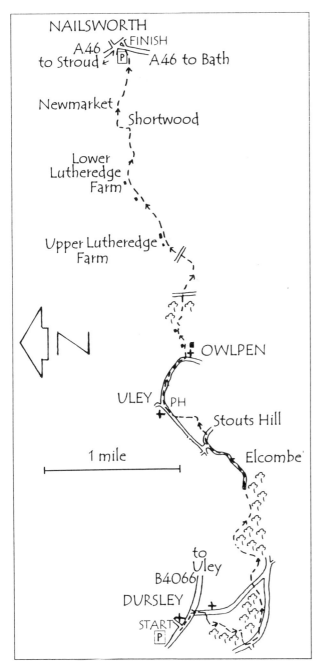

prominent hills on your left are Downham Hill and Uley Bury, the latter crowned by an Iron Age fort constructed around 300BC.

Reaching a T-junction at Stouts Hill, turn right then take the first footpath on the left, opposite the entrance to Stouts Hill Timeshare. The path leads beside the little River Ewelme until a footbridge allows you to cross the river. A well-trodden path climbs up a bank and takes you into Uley, a large village with some fine 18th-century houses testifying to its prosperity as a cloth centre before the Industrial Revolution. It was involved in the dyed-cloth industry and famous for "Uley Blue". Its zenith came during the Napoleonic Wars when demand for cloth for soldiers' uniforms soared dramatically (it is said the valley also sold cloth to the French) but hard times soon followed, with Uley unable to compete with the developing cloth towns of the North.

Keep forward to the main street and turn right. Pass the mainly Victorian church and then turn right past the pub on to Fiery Lane, which leads to Owlpen. Soon after you see a sign for Owlpen Manor, join the second footpath on the left, which leads to the church. There are glimpses of the manor from the churchyard but the classic view is from the south so take a path leading out of the churchyard and briefly join another footpath which runs in front of the manor to reveal one of the most famous scenes in the Cotswolds, with the 15th-century manor, its outbuildings and the Victorian church forming an immensely picturesque group in this hidden valley below wooded hills. The present house was probably begun about 1450 and was later extended and altered, but records show that the de Olepenne family was settled here as early as 1174, and remained in possession until 1464 when the manor passed to the Daunts, clothiers from Wotton-under-Edge. Owlpen is reputedly haunted by the ghost of Queen Margaret of Anjou, who is said to have stayed here before the Battle of Tewkesbury in 1471.

There is a fine group of manorial outbuildings, including a dovecote, mill, court house and barn and there are extensive formal gardens. It is a lovely place: as Edward Hutton writes in 1932 (*Highways and Byways in Gloucestershire*),"wandering in this far-off corner of the hills, the disaster of modern England can almost be forgotten." But even Owlpen has changed since Hutton's day, with visitors' cars detracting from the scene. There is holiday accommodation to let and the manor is open to the public (no dogs) from April to September (01453 860261).

When you've admired Owlpen, return to the track behind the church and follow it past a house, Manor Farm, and on towards another house, Woodwells. After passing Woodwells the track curves left and you should look out for a waymarked post indicating where a footpath leaves the track to climb steeply up a slope through beech, holly and yew woodland. Once at the top of the slope you emerge from the trees to rejoin the track. Cross it and go straight on, along the left-hand edge of an arable field.

Reaching a road, cross over and join another path which follows the left-hand edge of another arable field to a stile. Keep going along the left-hand edge of the next field until another stile gives access to a field on the left. Cross this and continue across an unfenced lane and on over another field to meet a bridleway near a house. Turn right and keep going past Upper Lutheredge Farm. Stay on the bridleway, which crosses pastureland, running along the top of a ridge, just to the right of a hedge at first. After passing to the right of a pair of modern barns, the bridleway descends to pass Lower Lutheredge Farm. When the track bends right, go over a stile to join a footpath which descends steeply to cross a dry stream-bed then contours around the side of a slope towards Nailsworth. Joining a track, turn right and walk to Shortwood, where you turn left on a track by The Old School House. This descends to cross Miry Brook and a right turn takes you through Newmarket to Nailsworth. When you reach Old Market a left turn leads to the bus station. To discover more about Nailsworth please turn to Walk 2.

Walk 9: Charlbury and Wychwood Forest

An easy circular walk in a pleasant and peaceful landscape with lovely woodland and a deer park. The footpaths are well maintained and easy to follow, with only three stiles.

Start/finish: Charlbury Station, grid reference 352195.

Length: 8½ miles/13.6km.

Maps: OS Landranger 164, OS Pathfinder 1091.

Refreshments: Pubs, coffee house and shops in Charlbury; pub at Finstock.

Buses: Worth's Motor Services Enstone/Chipping Norton to Oxford via Charlbury, Monday to Saturday; Enstone/Chipping Norton to Witney via Charlbury, Monday to Saturday.

Trains: Thames Trains and Great Western operate daily services on the Cotswold Line.

Parking: The car park at the station is meant for rail users, though there may sometimes be spaces available. There is a public car park in Charlbury.

Charlbury is a large village nestling snugly in the Vale of Evenlode on the eastern edge of the Cotswolds. Far from any of the major roads which cross the wolds, it has retained its rural air and has not fallen victim to mass tourism, despite being an attractive place with stone-built houses, shops and pubs and a welcoming coffee house which doubles as an art gallery.

Charlbury was probably settled quite early in the Anglo-Saxon period and seems to have quietly flourished ever since. It became a market town for a time and played its part in the wool trade, but later became known as a glove-making centre, using sheep skin and probably deer hide too. At the height of its prosperity in the 1850s the glove trade employed over 1000 people. The trade died out only comparatively recently and one 19th-century glove factory now serves as a youth hostel.

Exceedingly pleasant though Charlbury is, from the point of view of the walker its greatest asset is its setting on the edge of what was

The Oxfordshire Way at Charlbury

once one of England's largest Royal Forests. Centred on Burford, Wychwood Forest stretched from Rollright to Woodstock, from the Windrush to the Cherwell. Every English king from Ethelred the Unready to James I is said to have hunted there. It was famous for its deer and subject to extremely harsh Forest Law but the inhabitants of Burford enjoyed the right to hunt there on one day each year. As they also poached there the remaining 364 days it was claimed that Oxford Gaol was built mainly to house poachers caught in Wychwood.

Whatever the truth of that, it remains one of the best places in the Cotswolds for seeing deer today. Unfortunately, however, the forest went the way of most other Royal Forests and by the 19th century the great parks of Ditchley, Blenheim, Cornbury and Eynsham had been carved out of it, while most of the rest had been cleared for farming. Only a small area of the forest survives, ironically now just a part of the Cornbury Estate. Nevertheless, a new Wychwood Project has ambitious aims for the restoration of woodland cover.

Before you leave Charlbury Station have a look at the booking office, which was designed by Brunel and is a listed building. The station (and the town) featured in an episode of the BBC's detective drama *Dalziel and Pascoe* shown in 1997. The Cotswold Line was opened in 1853 by the Oxford, Worcester and Wolverhampton Railway Company, fondly known as the Old Worse and Worse, and later taken over by the Great Western Railway.

The Walk

Walk to the main road and turn left. When you reach the entrance to Walcot Farm, join the access road, which is also a bridleway and part of the Oxfordshire Way. After passing the farm the bridleway continues across wide fields with sweeping views over the rolling wolds until it brings you to Catsham Lane. Wychwood Forest is to the left, but first it's worth making a short detour to visit Shorthampton, which consists of a church, a farm and a couple of cottages. Just walk along the lane almost opposite to reach it.

All Saints' Church has been in existence for at least 800 years but little remains of the original building. Major alterations took place in the 15th century when the church was also decorated with a series

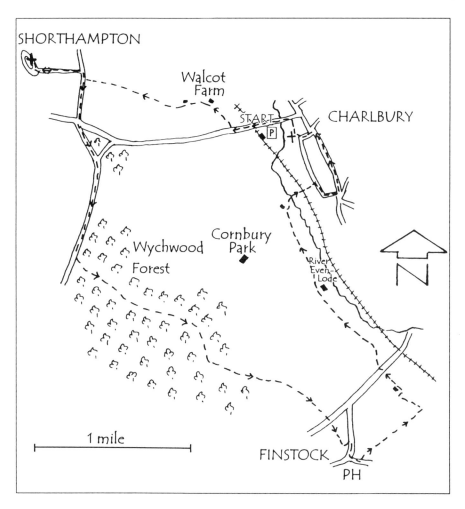

of wall paintings which, in the 16th century, were whitewashed over and replaced with biblical texts. It wasn't until major restoration work in 1903 that they were discovered. Unfortunately, the church is again in urgent need of repair. Much needs to be done, and the precious wall paintings are fading and disintegrating. One hundred thousand pounds are needed, and an appeal has been raised. Information about this may be found in the church, which is kept open for visitors.

Returning to Catsham Lane, turn right to the main road and cross to a lane opposite, where wide, grassy verges are backed by dense hedges festooned with wild clematis, and vibrant in autumn with the startling pink and orange fruits of the spindle tree and the red berries of bryony. Behind the hedges lie the beginnings of Wychwood Forest and from now on you can expect to see a variety of wildlife. Pheasants and squirrels are extremely common but muntjac deer are also quite numerous and can be surprisingly approachable. Fallow deer are present too, but are shyer than the muntjac.

At the next junction fork right, and before too long you'll see a stile on the left and a signpost for Finstock. This is where you enter Wychwood, which was once freely open to the public but has been forbidden territory for most of this century with past owners fighting hard to deny all access. In 1988 Oxfordshire County Council created a footpath through the forest and it has proved an immensely popular walk. The wide variety of trees you will see includes beech, oak, hazel, sycamore, field maple, ash, elm, hawthorn and elder, many of them draped with hanging curtains of wild clematis.

At a clearing the path turns right and continues to a junction by a pond, where you turn left. It climbs now, gently but steadily, and soon leaves the wood to continue as a tree-lined track for a while before the trees give way to grassland.

At the main road cross with care to a footpath opposite. A hedged, green lane which passes a chapel and leads to a housing estate, it then makes a left turn to emerge on a lane by the Old School House in Finstock. This rather fragmented village was, in the 1770s, visited three times by John Wesley, who wrote of its "delightful solitude". The chapel was built in 1841 on land given by the trustees of the Duke of Marlborough, and close to it is the grave of Jane, Baroness Churchill, who was Queen Victoria's maid and confidante for 46 years. She died in 1900.

Turn right along School Road, which soon descends to a junction where you turn left to the High Street and the Plough Inn, a thatched, stone building dating from 1732. Turn left, then left again on Dark Lane, a hedged track running between woods and fields. Ignore a branching footpath on the left and continue until the track makes a slight bend to the right. Turn left here, not over a stile but to the left of it, up an obvious path into a sloping field. After passing a solitary oak tree, turn right into the adjacent field and left along its edge, soon skirting a sewage works and joining a track to Charlbury Road. Cross to a footpath almost opposite which leads into Cornbury Park.

Cornbury originated as a royal hunting lodge in Wychwood Forest and many years later was given by Elizabeth I to her favourite, Robert Dudley, Earl of Leicester. Dudley died at Cornbury in 1588, allegedly from poison (possibly meant for his wife). In 1642 Charles I gave Cornbury to the Earl of Derby, and it later belonged to William Hyde, the Earl of Clarendon, Charles II's Lord Chancellor. Charles stayed at Cornbury, as did James II when he was still Duke of York, when he secretly married Anne Hyde, Clarendon's daughter. Cornbury Park Estate is now owned by Lord Rotherwick and part of it has been designated a National Nature Reserve because of its great variety of habitats. Cornbury House itself is a splendid 17th-century building surrounded by a beautiful deer park, where both red and fallow deer graze among monumental oaks and limes.

The footpath runs across farmland, then along an oak avenue and past a fishing pool to the entrance to the deer park. Pass to the right of a cattle grid and go forward along a path which follows the deer park's perimeter fence to North Lodge, where it turns right to the road. A glimpse of Cornbury House may be had through the splendid gateway by the lodge. Turn right when you reach the road and then turn left on Hixet Wood and follow it into Charlbury.

On your way back to the station you will pass the parish church, which is thought to have been founded in the mid-7th century by the Irish missionary bishop, St Diuma. An 11th-century document which lists the burial places of saints records that St Diuma "rests in the place that is called "Ceorlingburh" but no part of the present building is older than 12th century.

Walk 10: Tetbury and Westonbirt

*An easy, level, circular walk on good paths across pasture and parkland,
with some arable fields, too. It provides the opportunity to visit the
renowned Westonbirt Arboretum. An entrance fee is normally payable, but
walkers may explore part of the arboretum free of charge, using the
existing rights of way. Westonbirt is best avoided on October Sundays.*

Start/finish: The Market Place, Tetbury, grid reference 891931.

Length: 9 miles/14.5km.

Maps: OS Landrangers 173 or 162 and 163, OS Pathfinders 1133 and 1152.

Refreshments: Pubs, tea rooms, restaurants and shops in Tetbury; pub at
the crossroads near Westonbirt; outdoor (seasonal) café at Westonbirt Arboretum.

Buses: Stagecoach Stroud Valleys 29/30 from Stroud, Monday to Friday;
Andy James Coaches and Alex Cars from Cirencester, Kemble, Malmesbury
and Chippenham, Monday to Saturday.

Trains: Nearest station is Kemble.

Parking: Public car parks in Tetbury.

Tetbury is a classic Cotswold market town in the gentle countryside
of south Gloucestershire, close to the Wiltshire border, with wool
country to the north, dairy and arable lands to the south. This position made it a natural market centre, where, since the 13th century,
wool and cloth from the wolds, and dairy produce from Wiltshire
and the Vale of Berkeley have been traded. To add to the economic
strength of its position, the Market Square was laid out at the crossing point of roads to Bath, Cirencester, Swindon and Stroud. Tetbury became one of the main Gloucestershire centres for the sale of
woollen cloth, and even after the trade declined it continued to prosper thanks to its position on what had become important coaching
routes.

Unspoilt streets of 17th-, 18th- and 19th-century houses converge on the Market Square, dominated by the cupola-topped Market House, supported on sturdy stone columns and built in 1655 on
the site of an Elizabethan market hall. It used to have another storey

but this was removed during "renovations" in 1817. Despite the loss, it remains one of the finest buildings of its type in the Cotswolds.

To the south of the square is the graceful parish church, early Gothic Revival in style, mostly rebuilt between 1777 and 1781 on the site of a Norman predecessor. Perpendicular-style windows lend distinction to the exterior, and flood the elegant, fan-vaulted interior with light. The churchyard has an exceptional collection of headstones.

Though Tetbury enjoyed a mostly peaceful history, it was used as a base for the siege of nearby Malmesbury in the mid-12th century, when Empress Matilda was waging civil war against King Stephen. It had some sort of castle, but little is known about it and it may have been a very minor fortification. Very slight traces of earthworks survive just to the south of the church.

Tetbury is an excellent destination for anyone interested in antiques, with several good shops, though they do tend to be at the pricier end of the market: this has become a fashionable place to live since both Prince Charles and Princess Anne bought houses nearby. However, much cheaper antique fairs are sometimes held in the Market House. There are other attractive shops and the unusual Police Bygones Museum in the Old Court House.

Every Spring Bank Holiday Monday Tetbury remembers its past by staging a Woolsack Race, when opposing teams carry heavy woolsacks up and down steep (1in 4) Gumstool Hill during Tetbury Festival, while morris dancers, mummers and townsfolk dressed in medieval costume recreate something of the more colourful days of the past.

The Walk

Leaving the Market Place, walk down Silver Street (by the Snooty Fox) then turn left on Fox Hill, towards Malmesbury. Cross the Avon and join a footpath on the right. As you approach a sewage works there are two more footpaths on your right; join the left-hand one, which runs along field edges.

On reaching an avenue of trees, keep straight on but now on the other side of the hedge. At the bottom of the field go through a gate and turn left to cross a narrow field. Go through another gate, just past a young plantation, and follow the stream on your left to a foot-bridge. Cross over and walk alongside a field edge. After passing a stone stable, turn right to reach a lane, then right again for 300 me-tres.

Join a green lane (Wormwell Lane) on the left and follow it for about 600 metres until you reach a pair of hunting gates. Go through the one on the right and follow the left-hand wall to a gate then con-tinue along another green lane (Barber Lane). Turn left when you reach a road.

Pass the driveway to Elmestree House then join a bridleway on the left. Keep straight on to reach a lane then turn right to a cross-roads and look for an iron gate in the wall on the left, near a tree. Cross a field to a gate left of a copse and continue in the same direc-tion across another field.

Westonbirt School (formerly Westonbirt House) is now on your left, a flamboyant 19th-century neo-Elizabethan building designed by Lewis Vulliamy, who was also the architect of the Dorchester Ho-tel in London. Westonbirt House was the home of Robert Stayner Holford, who established the arboretum.

Maples at Westonbirt

You'll soon come to a junction of two metalled tracks. Join the one which takes you more or less straight on, to a lane at Westonbirt village, an estate village created in 1856. Turn right, then go straight on at a crossroads and again at the next junction to join a bridleway into Westonbirt Arboretum.

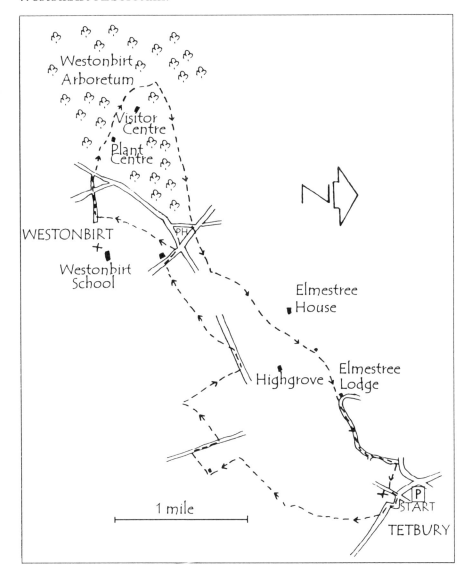

This was established in 1829 and acquired by the Forestry Commission in 1956. Almost 17 miles (27km) of paths thread through its huge area, much of which is semi-natural woodland. It is especially renowned for its maple collection, which attracts tens of thousands of visitors each autumn to see the spectacular colours.

Pass the Plant Centre and continue in the same direction, with Silk Wood, an ancient oakwood, on your left. When you cross a track near Waste Gate the Visitor Centre is uphill on the right, should you wish to buy an entrance ticket and explore more fully. Though it is most famous for its autumn display, Westonbirt has much to offer at any season. In spring there are masses of rhododendrons, azaleas, camellias, magnolias, flowering cherries and bluebells. The latter are at their best in Silk Wood, part of which is managed by Gloucestershire Wildlife Trust, which took over from the Forestry Commission in 1976. It's a typical, damp oakwood, with an understorey of ash, wild cherry, field maple and holly, and a healthy population of fallow deer.

When you reach a stile and a waymarked post you have the opportunity to follow the bridleway into Silk Wood if you wish. To return directly to Tetbury, however, turn right on a footpath up a slope. Go through a gate into farmland and walk along the outer edge of the arboretum, then straight on to a lane. The bridleway continues opposite, through a white gate. After about 500 metres, climb a stile on the left and cross two fields. Turn right along an enclosed track, pass to the right of a pond and continue along a field edge then straight across another field before bearing slightly left across parkland.

The house visible through the trees on your right is Prince Charles's home, Highgrove, built between 1796 and 1798 for the Pauls, a family of Huguenot extraction who became prosperous clothiers. The most famous member of the family was Sir George Onesiphorous Paul (1746-1820) a prison reformer whose memorial is in Gloucester Cathedral.

Cross the driveway of Elmestree House and keep on in the same direction to pass Elmestree Lodge, where you join Longfurlong Lane which leads back to Tetbury.

Walk 11: Mickleton, Hidcote and Ilmington

An undulating circular walk, with good paths through arable, pasture and woodland. There are about 15 stiles. If you wish to visit Hidcote Manor Garden it is best to avoid summer Sundays and bank holidays.

Start/finish: Mickleton, grid reference 161436.

Length: 9 miles/14.5km.

Maps: OS Landranger 151, OS Pathfinders 1020 and 1021, OS Outdoor Leisure 45.

Refreshments: Pubs and shop in Mickleton; tea bar and restaurant (seasonal) at Hidcote Garden; pubs in Ilmington.

Buses: Stagecoach Midland Red 21 "Cotswold Shuttle" Stratford to Bourton via Mickleton, daily; 22 Stratford to Broadway via Mickleton, Monday to Saturday; Castleways Coaches 569 Evesham to Moreton via Hidcote and Mickleton, daily except winter Sundays. Other less frequent services provided by Barry's, Cresswell's and Stagecoach Stroud Valleys operate from Moreton, Chipping Campden and Stroud.

Trains: Nearest station is Honeybourne.

Parking: Some roadside spaces available.

Regarded by some as the northernmost Cotswold village, Mickleton is not in itself particularly memorable, but it has an attractive situation beneath the hills and is a good starting point for some enjoyable walks. There are a number of fine buildings in the village, of which the most notable is probably St Laurence's Church, with its 14th-century tower and spire and unusual, 17th-century, two-storeyed porch.

The Walk

Starting in the village centre, take a "no through road" just after a phone box, passing the Manor and the church to join the Heart of England Way, which goes straight ahead, taking you into a field. Go diagonally right to the far corner, through a bridle gate and straight on by a field edge then along the edge of the next. Ignore a branching footpath on the right and keep following the hedge until a gate takes you into a large, sloping pasture. Follow a well-trodden path which climbs gently, veering slightly left up the slope. On the left, surrounded by fine trees, is Kiftsgate Court, whose celebrated garden is open to the public (01386 438777). The house itself is largely Victorian, but the garden was created after World War One by Heather Muir. It is renowned for its collection of old-fashioned roses, including the huge rambling rose *"rosa filipes Kiftsgate"*. The steep setting on the edge of the Cotswold scarp makes for a dramatic garden, which has continued to evolve under the care of Mrs Muir's daughter and granddaughter.

Go through another gate and keep climbing, aiming for a blue, wooden gate a little to the right of the imposing entrance gates to Kiftsgate. Join a lane at a junction and go straight ahead towards Hidcote Manor. The tree-lined lane climbs gently then levels out and leads to the car park for Hidcote. Our onward route is straight on, signed as "road used as public path", but first you may wish to visit Hidcote. Turn right if you do.

The 17th-century Hidcote Manor was acquired by Major Lawrence Johnston in 1905 and over the next 40 years he transformed the almost bare site into one of the most original and influential of 20th-century gardens. He made use of traditional cottage garden ideas and of the tenets of Gertrude Jekyll, but put his own very personal interpretation on them. Hidcote is designed as a series of small gardens separated by walls and hedges – in effect, a succession of surprise "rooms", each with its own atmosphere. It is famous for rare shrubs, trees, herbaceous borders, old roses and interesting species. Apart from the undoubted appeal of the garden itself, there are fine views to be enjoyed, too. Major Johnston gave the garden to the National Trust in 1948. (Admission details on 01386 438333.) A short distance from the garden is the hamlet of Hidcote Bartrim, a cluster of lovely cottages, several of them thatched.

Resuming the walk, however, return to the track and follow it uphill, enjoying good views of Broadway Hill, Bredon Hill and the Malverns. The track eventually makes a sharp right turn and then a sharp left, heading for three TV masts crowning Ebrington Hill, the

Hidcote Bartrim

highest point in Warwickshire (850ft/261m). Pass close by the masts and on to a lane, a former drove road.

Turn left, walking into a superb view of Warwickshire and ignoring two bridleways on the right as the lane descends to Lower Lark Stoke. On reaching a large sycamore by the entrance to a house, join the Centenary Way.

Pass to the left of the entrance gates, down an arable field and on towards a stile roughly halfway between two telegraph poles. Enter a pasture and bear right up a slope, more or less parallel with a brook which is below and to your right.

With a hedge on your left, continue to another stile. Climb over and turn right along the edges of two fields. The village of Ilmington comes into view now and there's another stile on the right. The path forks here but stay on the Centenary Way, which crosses the stile then goes diagonally left down the field. There are also green and white waymarkers here indicating a Countryside Stewardship site.

Go down the field, which is marked with medieval cultivation terraces, towards a group of pollarded willows, then climb up to the far top corner where there are two stiles. The first gives permissive access to another Countryside Stewardship site – limestone grassland which supports a variety of wild flowers in spring and summer.

Go over the second stile and diagonally left on the Centenary Way to the far corner of a large, rolling pasture. At the next stile the Centenary Way goes to the right – leave it here and go to the left, taking a fenced and hedged path down towards Ilmington.

This is probably the nearest Warwickshire has to a truly Cotswold village. Sheltered by the Ilmington Downs, its gracious buildings are a mixture of warm stone and mellow brick, with stone, tile and thatch roofs. Its name recalls the elms which once grew freely here, lining all the lanes, but which have long since fallen victim to Dutch Elm disease.

Reaching a cluster of buildings, take a left turn through a stable yard and down a well-defined path which brings you out opposite the 11th-century church of St Mary the Virgin, with its square tower and superb Norman doorway. Over the porch can be seen the coat of arms of Simon de Montfort, once patron of the church. The interior contains some fine memorials to local families and modern woodwork made in the 1930s by Robert Thompson of Kilburn, whose signature of a carved mouse occurs 11 times.

Turn right, then left on a lime avenue which skirts the churchyard. At the far side, by a cottage, turn left and soon right, passing between a pond (formerly a manorial fishpond) and a stone, timber and thatch house called Bevingtons. Turn left on another path which runs along the backs of some fine stone houses. When you come to a passageway on the right, take this to join the main street and turn right. Go straight on at a junction, soon passing Ilmington Pound, where stray animals used to be enclosed until claimed by their owners, who were liable to a fine. The practice declined after enclosure of the common fields in 1781.

Fork right past the village hall then left across the village green, passing to the left of the war memorial. Keep straight on along a "no through road" known as Grump Street, and past Crab Mill, one of the oldest houses in the village, dating from 1711. Its name refers to crab apples, not eight-legged crustaceans.

After passing Primrose Bank the road continues as a hedged,

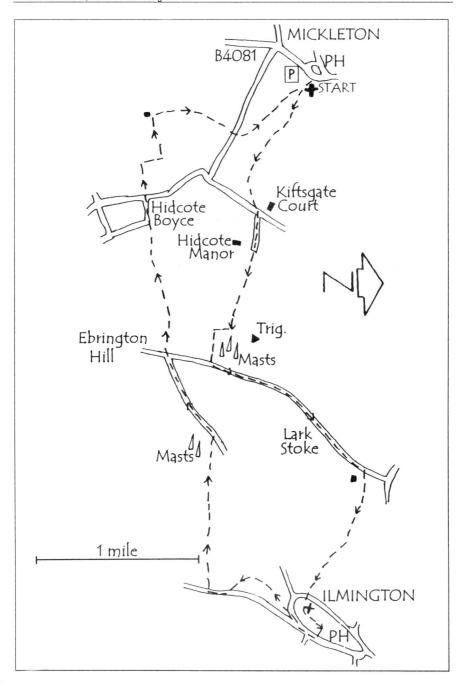

grassy track known as Tinker's Lane. Ignore all branching footpaths, continuing to a gate and stile at the end of the track. Go forward into a field as far as a drinking trough then turn left on a fairly well-trodden path which climbs a slope to a stile in the hedge at the top. Go straight across another field to a lane, where you turn right, climbing gently to meet a cross-track. Here you turn right again on a wide, hedged, stony bridleway known as Pig Lane. It climbs gently, providing marvellous views, then levels out when it reaches open, arable land. Continue towards two masts ahead, with Warwickshire on your right, the bosky Gloucestershire wolds on your left.

The track descends to meet a road where you turn left to walk up Ebrington Hill again. When you reach the old drove road, go through a gate to a footpath. The well-defined route runs straight ahead to the left of a wall at first, then diagonally left across hummocky pasture to join a farm vehicle track. This descends to Hidcote Boyce, a lovely hamlet with a single, sloping street bordered by flower-filled gardens.

Keep straight on through the village to a T-junction and join a footpath almost directly opposite. When you reach the end of an orchard and kitchen garden turn right, then soon left, descending a field and crossing a brook. Walk up the edge of the next field and then follow a track which passes to the right of a barn. Turn right on the Heart of England Way and follow it to the road, where you cross to a footpath opposite. Enter a pasture and go through a gate on the left then head towards Mickleton Church with a hedge on your right. After going through a gate in the far right-hand corner the path continues through woodland and on along the edge of pasture to Mickleton.

Walk 12: Chipping Norton and the Rollrights

Fine countryside, interesting villages and a notable ancient monument feature in this circular walk. Though the terrain is undulating it is relatively gentle and the paths are well-defined. There are about a dozen stiles.

Start/finish: The Market Place, Chipping Norton, grid reference 314271.

Length: 9½ miles/15.2km.

Maps: OS Landrangers 151 and 164, OS Pathfinders 1044 and 1068, OS Outdoor Leisure 45 shows part of route.

Refreshments: Pubs, tea rooms, restaurants, take-aways and shops in Chipping Norton; pub in Salford.

Buses: Stagecoach Midland Red X50 Oxford to Birmingham via Chipping Norton, daily; 487/488 Banbury to Chipping Norton, Monday to Saturday; 77 Moreton to Banbury via Long Compton, Thursdays and Saturdays; Stagecoach Oxford 20/20A/20B/20C Oxford to Chipping Norton, Monday to Saturday and probably summer Sundays; Barry's Coaches Moreton to Stratford via Long Compton, schooldays only; Worth's Motor Services Enstone to Oxford and Witney via Chipping Norton, Monday to Saturday. Many other less frequent services provided by Barry's, Baker's, Pulham's and Villager operate from all over the surrounding area.

Coaches: National Express 511 Great Malvern to London via Chipping Norton, daily.

Trains: Nearest station is Kingham.

Parking: Public car parks in Chipping Norton e.g. New Street.

The highest town in Oxfordshire, Chipping Norton stands on the eastern side of a valley carved by the River Swere, a tributary of the Evenlode. By the time of the Domesday Survey in 1086 Norton was already a sizeable community, but the prefix "Chipping", meaning market, was not acquired until the 13th century when the town was granted a charter for a weekly market and an annual fair. Chipping Norton soon grew rich on the proceeds of the wool trade and the wealth of the merchants is reflected in the fine buildings which throng the small town, though many of them were re-fronted in the

18th century, indicating that Chippy, as the locals call it, continued to prosper after the wool trade had passed its zenith, thanks to its position on a major coaching route.

The Walk

After exploring the town walk down New Street (the A44 towards Worcester) until you see an imposing building a few fields away to the left. This is Bliss Tweed Mill, built in 1872 in an elegant yet functional style with a balustraded parapet and a tall chimney rising from a domed tower. It was designed to resemble a great house in a parkland setting, but the chimney gives it away. It ceased production in 1980 and was later converted into flats.

On your right is a recreation ground where two footpaths are indicated. Join the one signposted to Salford, pass to the left of a fenced play area and descend towards the river. Once across, take the left-hand one of two footpaths, which goes straight up a field and across a track to another field before continuing gently uphill to the top left

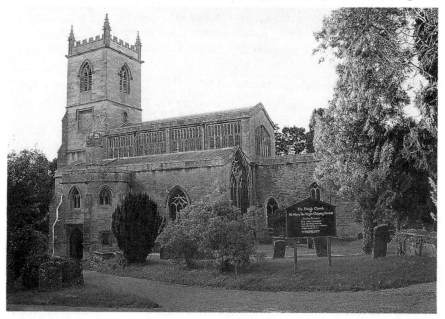

St Mary's Church, Chipping Norton

corner. Cross a stile, then turn right through a gap and immediately left along a field edge to the far corner.

Enter a huge, open field, enjoying the sudden panorama of Oxfordshire, Warwickshire and Gloucestershire which opens out

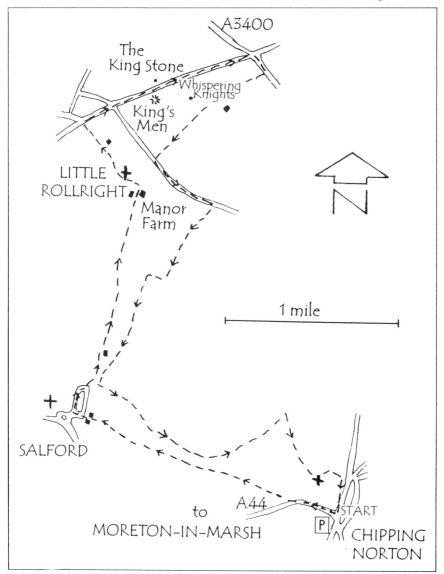

ahead. Go straight on and very soon the village of Salford comes into view. Head towards the left-hand edge of it on a just discernible path which leads to a stile in a hedge. Go forward to another stile then along the other side of the hedge on a farm track. Pass through Village Farm to enter Salford and go forward to a junction. The onward route is to the right, along Cooks Lane, but if you wish to visit St Mary's Church you should detour to the left. The original church on this site was erected in the Norman period but was rebuilt in the 1850s. The architect was George Street, later to become one of the foremost in his profession. Despite the rebuilding, some features from earlier centuries do survive and the north door (round the back) has an interesting tympanum.

Resuming the walk, follow Cooks Lane to a junction and turn left towards Rectory Farm. Ignore footpaths to left and right but then join the second left at a stile under a row of poplars. Go diagonally across a field to the next stile and bear left to another. Go straight on to enter Rectory Wood and pass through it to emerge at the far side. Continue along the edge of a field to the corner and through a gate into the field on the right. Keep going in the same direction on a clearly waymarked path. There are good views to the east before the path leads to Manor Farm at the hamlet of Little Rollright.

Pass through the farmyard to a junction then turn left along a lane to St Philip's Church, a simple and atmospheric little building which contains some hugely impressive memorials, particularly the canopied, marble chest tombs to members of the Dixon family. The church was much altered in the late 16th and early 17th centuries but examples of 13th-century work still survive, notably the chancel arch and windows.

Beyond the church join a footpath which climbs Baker's Hill to a barn then goes straight on to a road. Look back at this point to enjoy a fine view of the church in the context of its setting then turn right along the road.

This ancient ridgeway route, which offers fine views from its height of 710ft. (216 metres), forms the border between Oxfordshire and Warwickshire for the next mile or so, and is believed to have been part of one of Britain's earliest and most important tracks, the so-called Jurassic Way leading along the limestone belt from the Humber to Dorset.

When you reach a crossroads, keep straight on to visit the Rollright Stones, three separate prehistoric monuments. First to be seen, on the Oxfordshire side of the road, is the stone circle known as the King's Men, consisting of around 70 weather-worn, lichen-stained uprights. A little further on is the solitary King Stone. Taller than a man and weathered into an intriguing shape, the petrified king stands just inside Warwickshire, forever gazing north at the superb view. Further on again, in Oxfordshire, the Whispering Knights stand huddled, grey and lonely, in the middle of a field.

Nobody is quite certain what all these stones represent or even how old they are, but the general consensus is that the Whispering Knights, actually four uprights and a fallen capstone, are the remains of a burial chamber constructed in the Neolithic period, maybe 4000 years ago. The King's Men and the King Stone are probably Bronze Age, at least 3000 years old. They probably have ritual significance and may also be calendrical: a line taken from the centre of the circle through the King Stone points to the star Capella at the spring equinox, the time to sow. Alternatively, the King Stone may have been a marker for travellers approaching the circle.

The Rollrights seem to have always enjoyed considerable mystical significance, and in the Middle Ages peasants would chip pieces off to keep as charms against the Devil. Witches are reputed to have gathered here in Tudor times, and until comparatively recently local people used to meet at the stones once a year for dancing and drinking, perhaps continuing a long tradition of fertility rites. Today, battered and broken, the stones still cast a spell and New Age mystics dowse for ley lines and talk of fairies dancing round the King Stone, while strange sounds emanate from the Whispering Knights.

Legends abound, but the best-known concerns an ambitious king and his army, confronted here by a witch, Mother Shipton, who shrieked at the king:

> *Seven long strides thou shalt take*
> *And if Long Compton thou canst see*
> *King of England thou shalt be.*

As the King strode confidently forward to view the village of Long

Compton, which he knew to be below the ridge, he found it ob-
scured by a mound, and the witch cried:

> *As Long Compton thou canst not see*
> *King of England thou shalt not be.*
> *Rise up stick and stand still stone,*
> *For King of England thou shalt be none.*
> *Thou and thy men hoar stones shall be*
> *And I myself an eldern tree.*

The King was turned into the King Stone, of course, and his loyal
men became the stone circle, while a treacherous group, busy plotting his downfall, became the Whispering Knights. In an Arthurian
twist to the legend it is claimed that there is a great cave beneath the
King Stone in which he keeps watch. In England's hour of need the
spell will be broken and he and his men will hasten forth to defend
their country.

The Rollrights are privately owned but the public has been welcome to visit (on payment of a nominal fee which goes to animal
charities) over the last quarter century or so while the stones have
been in the care of Pauline Flick, who has resisted attempts to commercialise the site. However, she put them up for sale in 1997 and
much concern was generated about their future. Illusionist and psy-
chic Uri Geller was just one of those who expressed an interest in
buying the stones, which he believes have mystical powers and
stand on a ley line. Also interested was Julian Cope, former lead
singer with the 1980s band Teardrop Explodes. In the event, the
Rollrights were bought by two businessmen, who have apparently
pledged not to commercialise the site. Perhaps they will remove the
ugly railings which imprison the King Stone and the Whispering
Knights, diminishing their impact and atmosphere.

Having visited the Rollrights, continue to a crossroads. Turn right
here and join the first footpath on the right. This leads more or less
straight ahead over several fields, enabling you to view the Whispering Knights and the King's Men from another perspective, albeit a
more distant one, as you pass to the south of them. It brings you to a
lane overlooking Little Rollright.

Turn left along the lane until you come to a bridleway. This follows the left-hand hedge for a while before going diagonally across a

field to the far corner. Cross a brook and keep straight on by the right-hand field edge. Towards the end of the field bear left to find a gap in the hedge ahead and continue in much the same direction across another field. At the far side turn right to a bridle gate then left along a track to Salford.

Once back in the village, turn left to find a path signposted to Over Norton. A surfaced lane at first, it soon becomes a grassy track. Follow it for over a mile, ignoring the first footpath on the right but joining the second, which leads beside a hedge towards Chipping Norton. A well-trodden path, it soon changes to the other side of the hedge and continues towards Norton, passing the bumpy earth-works which are all that remain of a Norman motte-and-bailey cas-tle, then turning right to the church.

There was a stone church here at or soon after the Conquest and many of the stones from this early church must have been incorpo-rated into the fabric of the present building, which was greatly en-larged in the 14th and 15th centuries. The superb and very unusual hexagonal porch was probably built at this time and an appealing legend tells that it was intended to commemorate the casting out of five devils from the church in 1302 by a priest named Henry of Winchcombe. Certainly there are five grotesque heads carved on the ceiling. Henry is said to have pursued the devils to the market place where he lost them in a flock of sheep.

Outside, the churchyard is pleasantly leafy and contains some in-teresting headstones, including an unusual one in memory of Phillis Humphreys, an itinerant rat catcher. You'll find it close to the path on the south side of the church.

Church Street, Church Lane or Diston Lane all offer attractive routes back to the town centre, but choose Church Street if you would like to see a row of gabled almshouses dating from 1640, the gift of Henry Cornish for poor widows "of honest and Godly life and conversation".

Walk 13: Painswick and Slad

This is a beautiful circular walk in an area characterised by beech-covered hills, deep valleys and narrow, winding lanes. There are 15 stiles and a few climbs, some quite steep, but always brief in duration. Painswick is best avoided on summer weekends.

Start/finish: Painswick Church, grid reference 866097.

Length: 9½ miles/15.3km.

Maps: OS Landrangers 162 and 163, OS Pathfinder 1113.

Refreshments: Pubs, tea rooms, restaurant and shops in Painswick; The Woolpack at Slad.

Buses: Stagecoach Stroud Valleys 46 Cheltenham to Stroud via Painswick, Monday to Saturday. (Stagecoach buses 10, 50 and 52 from Gloucester connect with the 46 at Brockworth). Beaumont Travel operates some services from Gloucester direct to Painswick, Monday to Saturday.

Trains: Nearest station is Stroud.

Parking: Public car park on Stamages Lane, off the A46 south of the church.

Not for nothing is Painswick known as Queen of the Cotswolds. Even monarchs have been impressed by its rural charms – it was Charles I who, in 1643, gave the name Paradise to a small hamlet less than a mile to the north. Charles was staying there during the Civil War while engaged in his unsuccessful attempt to take Gloucester, and one can only hope he found some solace in the tranquillity which surrounded him. Other Royal visitors charmed by Painswick include Henry VIII and Anne Boleyn who spent a couple of days there in those happy months before Henry decided Anne would be improved by the removal of her head.

The little town perches on a high spur between two valleys close to where the Cotswold escarpment plunges towards the Vale of Gloucester. Narrow lanes tumble into the valley of Painswick Stream, which is straddled by several former mills, once used in the production of cloth, but now converted into houses. At its peak in the 18th century there were at least 30 mills on Painswick Stream and its tributaries.

Painswick, which benefited from both the wool trade and the dyed-cloth industry, is packed with beautiful buildings. A 14th-century house on Bisley Street still has a "donkey door", wide enough to allow a fully laden donkey to pass through. On New Street is one of Britain's most attractive post offices, featured in 1997 on a Royal Mail commemorative stamp. A 15th-century, timber-framed house, it is said to be the oldest building in England from which post office services are provided. Most houses, however, are of stone, and date from the 17th and 18th centuries, when the prosperous cloth-iers were building themselves new homes. The stone was quarried locally and is much paler than most Cotswold stone; in certain lights it looks almost silver.

St Mary's Church sends its tall spire soaring skyward above a magnificent churchyard, planted in 1792 with avenues of yew trees,

Lychgate, Painswick Church

said to be 99 in number. Legend has it that if a hundredth is planted the Devil kills it, but there are more than that. In fact, there are so many that it would probably qualify as a wood if each was not meticulously clipped into a severely architectural shape. Sombre and formal, the yews watch over the best collection of 17th- and 18th-century tombs in the country, many of them embellished with classical ornamentation. Though most are table tombs, others are of the unusual "tea caddy" type with the emphasis on vertical design.

The Walk

Walk through the churchyard, emerging at the rear of it into a little square of lovely houses. Close by stand the village stocks, installed in 1840, and of a type known as spectacle stocks because of their shape. They are unusual in being made of cast iron: in fact, there are said to be only two such specimens in existence. Go down Hale Lane which descends steeply, bordered by more lovely old houses, to a T-junction. Turn right and keep going along Knap Lane, which also descends steeply. Just after passing Knap Cottage, as the lane bends right, go straight ahead instead, on a footpath down to Painswick Stream.

Cross the stream and turn right as the lane becomes a muddy track. Ignore a footpath on the left and stay on the track as it bends to the right. When it forks take the left-hand branch, a hedged, green lane which often runs with water. Bordered by hart's-tongue fern, holly and ivy, it climbs to a stile. Go straight on along the edges of paddocks to a track and continue to a lane. Turn left, soon passing the eccentric Red Stables before you fork right, signposted to "Bulls X".

Bulls Cross is a tiny common at a meeting of ancient roads where a gibbet once stood. This open grassland and encroaching woodland is a marvellous place for wild flowers in the spring, with sheets of yellow leopard's bane in May being particularly notable.

At a fiveways junction turn right on a track then soon right again on a bridleway into Gloucestershire Wildlife Trust's Frith Wood. Also known as the Morley Penistan Memorial Reserve, after a former Chairman of the Trust, the wood contains mature beeches grown from seed planted after the Napoleonic Wars. While beech dominates the canopy, other species also thrive, including ash, oak, sycamore, holly, yew, whitebeam and field maple. The ground flora includes uncommon species such as white helleborine and columbine.

Keep to the main bridleway which climbs gently through the wood. When it levels out you come to a glade and the bridleway forks. Take the left branch which descends the eastern slope of the ridge. Ignore any branching paths, and keep going to the edge of the

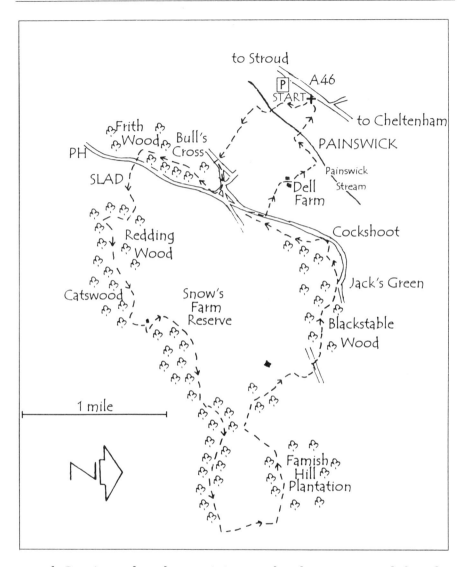

wood. Continue along here to join a track, where you turn left to descend to Slad Road.

The straggling hillside village of Slad, just to your right, is where the writer Laurie Lee was born in 1914. His autobiographical *Cider with Rosie*, published in 1959, is a loving evocation of life in the Slad valley in the 1920s and should be read by everyone who loves this countryside. Lee spent much of his life here, living in later years at Little Court, close to The Woolpack, where he was a regular. Today a plaque marks the place where he sat and drank, often with his friend and fellow poet Frank Mansell, who is known for his *Cotswold Ballads*. Laurie Lee died in 1997 and is buried at the village chapel.

Cross the road and go down the lane almost opposite, by the war memorial. Just after Rose Cottage the lane makes a sharp bend to the right then descends steeply to a junction with Steanbridge Lane. Our onward route is to the left, but you may first wish to make a short detour into Slad.

Otherwise, turn left. After passing a former mill pond and an adjacent wooded area, turn right on a deeply sunken track, which is host to a stream and climbs between banks of hart's-tongue and holly to enter Redding Wood. At a crosstracks keep climbing. When the track levels out, turn sharp left on another which runs along the top edge of the wood before cutting through it to end up by the bottom edge of adjacent Catswood. There are lovely views across a valley to Snow's Farm, another GWT reserve. Containing unimproved limestone grassland, ancient woodland, scrub and a stream, this reserve protects a varied range of habitats and an area of high scenic value. The limestone grassland contains an excellent range of wild flowers, including fragrant orchid, autumn gentian and clustered bellflower. Access is by permit only, except on the rights of way which enter the reserve.

When you come to a gate turn left down a sunken lane, descending steeply to cross a brook and then climbing up the other side of the valley to a T-junction just below a house. Turn right, then soon left past a breeze-block garage. Climb steeply to another junction and take the second left, immediately plunging into more woodland.

The path descends to another junction where you turn right for a few paces, entering the GWT reserve. Go down steps and continue to a stile, where a sign requests that dogs be on a lead at all times. Cross the stile and turn right above a steep valley. Another stile takes you back into woodland and the path continues in the same direction, soon passing through an area of scrub on the side of a slope, then gradually descending so that it runs alongside Dillay Brook. It eventually joins a partially walled and hedged green lane where you turn left, passing a cottage. Just beyond this there's a stile – ignore it and stay on the sunken track, which keeps climbing between holly-covered banks then continues as a wide path along the edge of woodland. It soon begins to bear right a little as it climbs. Fork left as you approach a house, so that you walk below it through the woods. The path then bends right and climbs to a junction. Turn left on a track which continues through woodland before eventually emerging into fields.

Keep forward for a short distance until a stone wall on your left comes to an end. Turn left here and follow the hedge to a stile then bear slightly right, following overhead power lines and a succession of waymarked stiles to reach a track which runs beside a row of pines and larches. Turn left, soon entering Famish Hill Plantation. Fork right at a junction and at the next fork right again, but almost at once climb a stile on the left which takes you into a narrow, grassy valley enclosed by woodland.

Bear right to where a spring issues from the ground and follow the ensuing stream, Dillay Brook, keeping to the right of it. Before long you'll pass another spring then climb over a sort of stile and continue in the same direction until you come to a signposted junction. Turn right up a bank and into a wood. Bear left on a rising path, cross another and keep climbing to reach a stone stile in a tumbledown wall. Cross over into a field and follow its right-hand edge to a track. Continue in the same direction to pass Down Barn Farm and reach a T-junction. Turn right to the road and then left.

Cross over and take the first footpath, an unsigned green lane which leads into Blackstable Wood National Nature Reserve. Follow the bridleway down into the wood until you come to a junction. Continue in the same direction along the lower edge of the wood, with a view of Sheepscombe below. Go right at the next junction, still along the edge. Continue forward to leave the wood at Jack's Green. Turn left by a cream-coloured bungalow and return to the wood, forking right along its edge.

Leave the wood again at Cockshoot Common and follow a track past houses until you can join another footpath on the left, so that again you're walking along the woodland edge. Leave it at a stile and continue forward past more houses. After the last one turn right over grassland to a lane, and right again until you see a footpath on the left, a green lane which leads to Dell Farm. Turn right through the farmyard, then left after a stable block. Walk down to a mill by Painswick Stream and turn left. Before long a stile and steps take you closer to the stream, which you follow to a lane before turning right by Brookhouse Mill and up steeply rising Tibbiwell into Painswick. As you climb the hill, look for the stream issuing forth from Tibby Well, also known as St Tabitha's Well, which gives Tibbiwell its name.

Walk 14: Stroud and Bisley

An undulating circular walk with lots of short, sharp slopes. Scenically superb, with mainly pasture and woodland. There are 18 stiles.

Start/finish: The High Street, Stroud, grid reference 852052.

Length: 10 miles/16km.

Maps: OS Landranger 162 and 163, OS Pathfinder 1113.

Refreshments: Shop and pubs in Bisley; pubs, cafés, tea rooms, restaurants, take-aways and shops in Stroud.

Buses: Stagecoach Stroud Valleys 16 Uley and Dursley to Stroud, Monday to Saturday; 46 Cheltenham to Stroud, Monday to Saturday; 77 Swindon to Stroud, Monday to Saturday; 90/92/93 Gloucester to Stroud, Monday to Saturday; other less frequent Stagecoach services from Cirencester, Tetbury, Minchinhampton, Wotton under Edge, Charfield, Kingswood etc. (If you should want to cut the walk short, buses 23 and 25 run from Bisley to Stroud.)

Coaches: National Express 335 Halifax to Bournemouth via Stroud, daily; 339 Birmingham to Bristol via Stroud, daily; 503 Hereford to London via Stroud, daily.

Trains: Great Western and Wales and West operate daily services to Stroud on the Paddington – Swindon – Gloucester – Cheltenham line, and some services also operate direct to/from Worcester.

Parking: Public car parks in Stroud.

Five valleys converge on Stroud, which by the 15th century had already established itself as the main centre of the Cotswold cloth industry. At its peak in the 18th and early 19th centuries there were over 150 mills operating in the valleys and Stroudwater Scarlet, used for military uniforms, became internationally famous. In the 19th century, competition, first from the Pennines, then from abroad, led to the closure of most of the mills. Only a handful are still working today but Stroud remains a lively place, colourful, characterful and cosmopolitan, populated by independent thinkers and individualists, with a flourishing "alternative" culture and one of the highest concentrations of artists and craftspeople in Britain. The main valleys are still busy as other industries have moved in, but the smaller valleys, to the north and east, are beautiful, tranquil places, rich in wildlife. This walk heads quickly out of town to the "jungly, bird-crammed, insect-hopping woodland" so evocatively portrayed by Laurie Lee in *Cider With Rosie*.

The Walk

Walk to the top of the High Street, across the main road and on along Nelson Street. At a fork keep straight ahead on Castle Street then fork left on Lower Street, which leads to the junction of Field Road, Bowbridge Lane and Trinity Road. Turn left on the latter, past a church and then right on Horns Road. At a junction with Spider Lane, carry straight on along a "no through road". This descends slightly to Horns Farm, where you join a footpath threading through the trees on the left to reach a stile.

After emerging from the trees, the well-trodden path continues along the top edge of a field to another stile then continues in the same direction along the side of a narrowing valley. A stile gives access to the next field, across which you go diagonally right, stepping across a stream and proceeding to the top edge of the wood on the other side. Cross a stile and turn right up a scrub-covered bank. Follow the right-hand fence to a stile, cross over this and an adjacent one then continue up the bank, joining the drive of Woodland Cottage which takes you up to a track. Follow it to a road.

Turn left briefly, then right on to a "no through road" which leads to Middle Lypiatt House. Continue past the house and go forward past a cottage to a gate where two footpaths are indicated. Take the one which forks left, a well-trodden route descending a thistly, scrub-dotted field towards Toadsmoor Valley, a deep and secluded wooded combe which runs from the Golden Valley at Brimscombe almost to Bisley. After a steep, uneven descent the path makes a left turn past an idyllically situated cottage and heads towards the valley, descending beside a brook which flows from the cottage garden.

Holly, hazel, maple, beech and yew line the path and meet overhead, creating a leafy tunnel. Descend to the valley floor and turn left to pass Toadsmoor Pond. At the next junction keep more or less straight on to pass Keeper's Cottage. Continue by the woodland edge, with a stream and freshwater springs on your right. When you

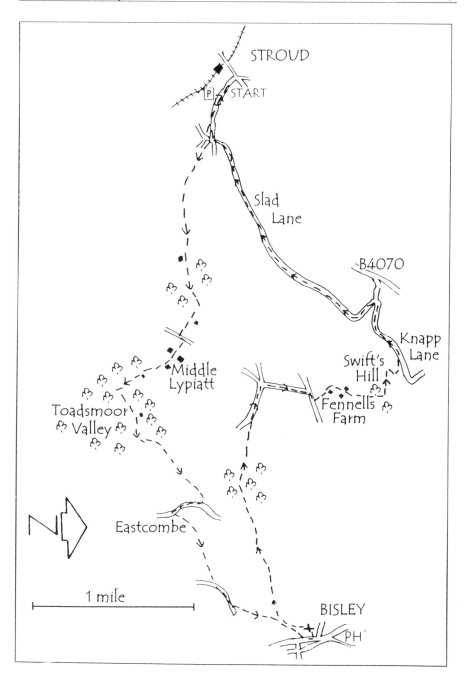

STROUD

START

Slad
Lane

B4070

Knapp
Lane

Swift's
Hill

Middle
Lypiatt

Fennells
Farm

Toadsmoor
Valley

Eastcombe

1 mile

BISLEY

PH

Toadsmoor Valley

reach a junction with a rough lane turn right, crossing the brook, then turn left just before a house. A walled, tree-lined green lane climbs to a junction with another. Turn left just above Little Bismore Cottage and walk through woods of beech, holly and hazel to reach a waymarked junction. Keep straight ahead, and do the same again at the next junction, ignoring a path branching left into the wood. Emerge from the trees on a track near some houses and keep going in the same direction.

By the access track to Hawkley, turn right up a rough lane and join the second footpath on the left, just as you reach the edge of Eastcombe. Take a well-trodden route across fields towards Bisley, whose tall church spire is a useful landmark.

On reaching a lane turn left past a handful of farms and cottages, one of which is named Packman's Way, recalling the days when these lanes were trodden by trains of packhorses carrying bales of cloth. Join a footpath on the left here, just opposite a cottage. Cross to the far corner of a field, passing beneath some large oak trees to reach a gate which gives on to a green lane. At a junction with a surfaced lane turn left, and when you reach Hartwell Cottage turn right to the centre of Bisley.

A huddle of cottages arranged in seemingly haphazard fashion around a maze of steep, narrow lanes and tracks, Bisley is largely the product of the boom years of the cloth trade, during which wealthy clothiers built fine houses for themselves. Interesting buildings include 16th-century Wesley House, where the founder of Methodism sometimes stayed, and the Bear Inn, which was formerly the court house, with its upper floor supported on stone pillars. Not far from the Bear is an unusual gabled lock-up with two cells, dated 1824.

Make your way to the churchyard. There has been a Christian church here since Saxon times, and possibly a pagan temple before that for two Roman altars were found during restoration work in the 19th century. The present church was rebuilt in 1862 but retains its medieval tower and chancel. One of the main features of interest inside is the font, which was made in around 1200 and is unique in having two fish carved inside the bowl.

Outside the church, not far from the main door, is a tall stone structure which is actually a lantern-like well head dating from the

12th or 13th century. It was used as a poor souls' light, housing candles lit for masses for the poor, and it is known locally as the Bonehouse because it covers a well into which a priest apparently fell to his death one dark night about 600 years ago. It is said to be the only outdoor poor souls' light in England.

From the Bonehouse walk forward to the stone wall which bounds the churchyard and turn left along a lime avenue before descending a flight of steps to a lane. Our onward route is to the right but first have a look at the spring-fed, duck-frequented wells on the left. Known as Seven Springs or Bisley Wells, this may have been a sacred site in pagan times, which would explain why there was a Roman temple where the present church stands. The gabled water chutes and stone tanks were restored by Thomas Keble, Vicar of Bisley from 1827 until 1873, and every Ascension Day they are dressed with flowers by the village children in a ceremony initiated by Keble in 1863.

Turn left on a bridleway by a cottage named Pax. Pass Hartwell Cottage to return to where you earlier entered the village, but fork right up a gently rising hill. The path is unmistakable as it climbs and enters open fields. Just keep straight on along a field edge with a wooded slope falling steeply away on your left.

When you see a stile on the left enter a pasture and descend past a large, solitary tree, then to the left of a fenced copse, enjoying an enticing view of the Golden Valley ahead. Pass to the right of a second copse and continue across the pasture, guided by a line of sycamores and oaks, before heading towards the far left corner where a stile gives access to beechwoods. Descend to the floor of the valley, cross a brook and go straight on up a grassy bank towards another wood (mainly sycamore). A stepped path climbs quite steeply through the trees to a stile and straight on to the top of the bank and along the edge of the next field to a road.

Turn right, then right again at a crossroads. Turn right once more at the next junction and cross to a footpath on the left, opposite the castellated lodge at the entrance to Lypiatt Park. Pass Fennells Farm then swing right on a stony, fenced track which leads through a former farmyard. Cross a garden to a stile in the fence ahead and bear right across rough pasture to the far right corner. The path enters woodland before reaching a stile giving access to a Gloucestershire Wildlife Trust nature reserve christened Elliott by the Trust after a past owner, but better known as Swift's Hill. Go straight on through the wood to the open limestone grassland which covers most of Swift's Hill.

The footpath, terraced into the hillside, runs above a tremendously steep slope which falls away on your left. There are lovely views ahead and Stroud is now visible to the south. Though unregistered, Swift's Hill is regarded as common land and is unfenced. Its commons status and steep slopes have combined to save it from cultivation or so-called "improvement" with fertilisers. As a result it is rich in wild flowers, including 11 species of orchid. There are masses of cowslips in the spring and other notable species include columbine and autumn gentian. The flowers attract many butterflies, with 29 species recorded so far, as well as colourful day-flying moths such as cinnabar and six-spot burnet. The warm south- and west-facing slopes with their short turf and stony soils provide a good habitat for snakes and lizards, though it takes luck and patience to see these elusive animals.

The path bears right, keeping to the perimeter of the reserve, and descends past old quarry workings, now full of wild flowers, to Knapp Lane, where you turn left. At a junction turn left again and follow Slad Lane into Stroud.

Walk 15: Moreton-in-Marsh and Chastleton

A level and easy circular walk in the pleasant Vale of Evenlode, with a spectacular Jacobean house as the focal point. There are only a few stiles but you may find some paths slightly overgrown, though not enough to impede progress.

Start/finish: Moreton-in-Marsh Station, grid reference 206327.

Length: 10 miles/16km.

Maps: OS Landrangers 151 and 163, OS Pathfinders 1044 and 1068, OS Outdoor Leisure 45.

Refreshments: Pubs, tea rooms, restaurants, take-aways and shops in Moreton.

Buses: Castleways Coaches 569 Cotswold Explorer Evesham to Moreton, daily except winter Sundays; Stagecoach Midland Red 21" Cotswold Shuttle" Stratford to Bourton via Moreton, daily; Pulham's Coaches Cheltenham, Bourton and Stow to Moreton, daily except winter Sundays. For other less frequent services to Moreton, please see Walk 6.

Coaches: National Express 511 Great Malvern to London via Moreton, daily.

Trains: Thames Trains and Great Western operate daily services to Moreton on the Cotswold Line.

Parking: Public car park next to the railway station.

The Fosse Way passes through Moreton and forms its broad High Street, lined with elegant buildings, mostly of the 17th, 18th and 19th centuries, though the oldest building in town is the Curfew Tower at the corner of Oxford Street, dating from the 16th century. A bell was tolled for the curfew until 1860, its purpose to warn householders to cover their fires, a necessary precaution when so many buildings contained exposed timbers which might be set alight by stray sparks. On the wall is a fascinating list of market tolls, dated 1905. Today, Moreton is still at its liveliest on a Tuesday when a traditional street market brings in shoppers from far and wide. For further information about Moreton, please see Walk 6.

The Walk

Leave the station, go down Station Road and cross Oxford Street (which can also be reached direct from the High Street). Descend a flight of steps and go straight on. Pass the churchyard then cross Grays Lane and keep forward until a left turn is indicated. After passing allotments turn right on to a footpath and keep straight on, crossing a residential street before making a left turn along the edge of a field. A short distance on a footbridge gives access to a clear path running across the field. When the path joins a track, continue in the same direction. After crossing a footbridge, turn left over another bridge and a stile. Bear right towards a farm, passing through a series of gates which guide you to the left of it. Continue past a new house to join a grassy path.

The route is now obvious until the path is crossed by a bridleway. Turn left here, eventually crossing the River Evenlode and the railway before joining a green lane. Follow it to a waymarked post where you turn right on a cross-field footpath. Keep the same heading for half a mile, passing a barn and entering a cow pasture. Towards the far end of the pasture two stiles give access to another field. Keep left to reach a lane then turn right into Evenlode. This attractive village in lush meadowland was part of Worcestershire but surrounded on all sides by Gloucestershire until actually acquired by the latter in 1931. It has a Georgian rectory, several lovely farmhouses and a village green. The church was badly restored by the Victorians but some late Norman work survives, notably the chancel arch. One unusual feature is a millstone once used to grind flour for communion wafers. A fragment of ancient glass depicts Edward the Confessor, to whom the church is dedicated. When you first reach the T-junction at the edge of the village you can turn either left or right as the lane is circular. Our onward route is Horn Lane, a "no through road" which leaves Evenlode at the south-east corner of the village. If you want to visit the church you should go to the right; if you want to see the green go to the left. A little retracing of steps, of course, will allow a more complete exploration. At any rate, once you join Horn Lane the route is obvious, passing a few farms before the lane becomes a farm track and bridleway. As you pass Harcomb

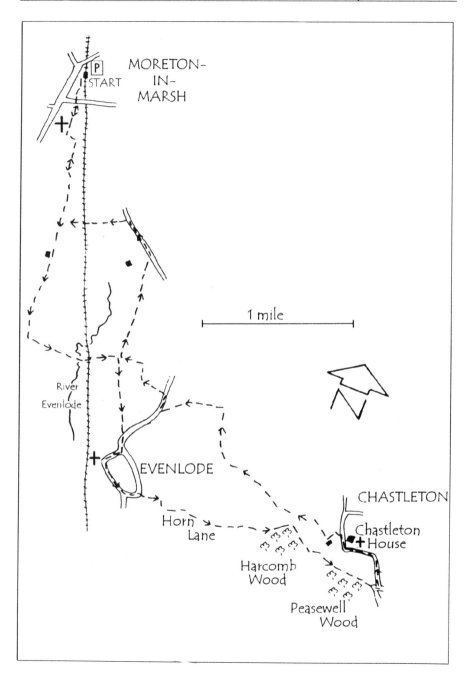

Wood the track veers left but you should stay on the bridleway, close to the wood, so as not to miss a sharp right turn at the corner ahead.

This takes you on to a green track, Conygree Lane, with Chastleton House now visible on your left. Keep straight ahead, soon passing Peasewell Wood, to reach a lane below Chastleton Hill. Two left turns here will take you to Chastleton itself, a tiny village in a finger of Oxfordshire squeezed between Gloucestershire and Warwickshire. Chastleton House is the dominating feature, a battlemented and gabled early Jacobean mansion which has been preserved for nearly 400 years in the style in which it was first built.

The first family known to have lived on this site were the Trillowes in the 14th century. They were succeeded by the Catesby family, one of whom, William, was one of Richard III's most unpopular ministers. A later member, Robert, was shot dead while resisting arrest for his part in the Gunpowder Plot of 1605, but before this he had already been implicated in plotting against the king, for which he was fined heavily, as a result of which the family had to sell the Manor of Chastleton in 1602. The purchaser was Walter Jones, a

Chastleton House

wealthy lawyer and former wool merchant from Witney. He started building a new house in 1607 and it was more or less complete by 1612. The house remained in the ownership of his family, or branches of it, until 1991, when it came into the hands of the National Trust.

One of England's finest and most complete Jacobean houses, it is suffused with the atmosphere of nearly 400 years' occupation by one family. Virtually unchanged, it retains many of its original furnishings, but was in a sorry state when taken over by the National Trust. It could have easily been ruined by heavy-handed restoration but the Trust worked with sensitivity, over a six-year period, to ensure the survival of its spirit as well as its fabric. Chastleton opened to the public in 1997, but because the protection of the house is the overriding concern, visitor numbers are controlled, with all entry by pre-booked, timed ticket (01608 674284). The exterior can be admired at any time from the lane.

Chastleton's history has been largely uneventful, except for the aftermath of the Battle of Worcester in 1651 when Arthur Jones returned home to his wife with a troop of Roundheads in hot pursuit, believing him to be Charles II. He hid in a secret room off the main bedroom while the soldiers searched the house. They then decided to stay the night in the Jones's bedroom so Arthur's wife, Sarah, spiked their wine with laudanum. While they slept he crept past them and once he reached the stables selected the best of their horses to make his escape.

Next to the house is St Mary's Church, which was begun around 1100. All that remains from that period are the Norman doorway and some arched pillars, and possibly the font. One of the church's main treasures is a collection of glazed medieval floor tiles, dating from the 14th century, on the floor of the south aisle chapel. On the north wall of the church are traces of wall paintings, first uncovered in the 1930s and thought to be examples of 17th- or 18th-century work. In 1878 another wall painting was reputedly discovered but it depicted the Last Judgement in such horrifying detail that it was hastily covered over again by the susceptible Victorians.

Having admired church and house, continue along the lane as far as a postbox then join a "no through road" which passes several cottages before turning sharp right as you approach a farm. Now a bridleway, the track runs for nearly a mile before reaching a junction. Keep straight on, passing through a gate into a field and following its right-hand edge. After leaving the field a short length of green lane leads to a gate. Pass through and turn left to reach a road. Turn right, then shortly left on a bridleway. After a third of a mile climb a stile on the right (opposite the point where you left this bridleway on the outward leg) and walk across three fields then a little way along the left-hand edge of a fourth before turning left over a stile. Cross a narrow field to enter a much larger one. Two paths are signposted here – take the one which goes diagonally to the road. Turn left for about 400 metres then join a path on the left, signposted to Evenlode. This rejoins the path on which you left Moreton and it is now only a mile or so back to the town centre.

Walk 16: Naunton and Guiting Power

*A lovely circular walk on clear paths through woodland and mixed
farmland, with some gentle slopes but no real hills and only a few stiles. It
visits three very different villages and samples both the Wardens' Way
and the Windrush Way.*

Start/finish: St Andrew's Church, Naunton, grid reference 113233.

Length: 10½ miles/16.8km.

Maps: OS Landranger 163, OS Pathfinder 1067, OS Outdoor Leisure 45.

Refreshments: Pubs and shops in Naunton and Guiting Power; pub on the
Cheltenham road near Naunton.

Buses: Pulham's Coaches Moreton to Cheltenham call at Naunton on Saturdays only, on other days get off at the Hawling turn (1 mile from Hawling); Pulham's Temple Guiting to Cheltenham and Guiting Power to Bourton services
offer some possibilities but are of limited use to most people; Villager operates occasional buses from Oddington and Stow to Naunton.

Trains: Nearest stations are Cheltenham and Moreton.

Parking: Near Naunton church, but please be considerate. There is also a
small car park by a crossroads near a ford on Critchford Lane between Guiting Wood and Guiting Power, grid reference 084259.

Naunton is a long, narrow village strung out along the banks of the
Windrush in a deep valley below the high road from Cheltenham to
Stow. It has lots of delightful cottages, a 17th-century dovecote with
four steeply pitched gables and 12th-century St Andrew's Church,
rebuilt in the 16th century and restored in 1878. Don't miss the fine
gargoyles and two unusual 18th-century painted sundials adorning
its Perpendicular tower.

Naunton was once a quarrying centre specialising in roofing
slates, of which up to 30 000 a week were produced. Many Oxford
colleges are roofed with Naunton slate (a local term for what is actually split stone). The quarrying revealed how rich in fossils the local
stone is and many of Naunton's window sills and garden walls are
decorated with brachiopods, ammonites and the like. The teeth of a
plesiosaur and the jawbone of a megalosaurus have been found at a
nearby quarry.

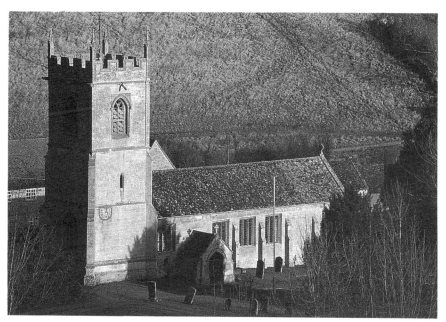

St Andrew's Church, Naunton, from the south

The Walk

When you've explored the village, walk through the churchyard to a lane and turn right to reach the Cheltenham road. Go straight ahead at a crossroads and follow the road to the Foxhill Inn, then pass between large stone gateposts to join an unclassified road.

At Tally Ho Farm fork left on a bridleway which soon merges with the Windrush Way. Keep straight on along a pleasant valley to reach Hawling Lodge where, if you wish, you may explore a grassland site open to the public under the Countryside Stewardship scheme. An information board and map provide details.

To continue the walk, follow the road past the lodge and you'll see the Windrush Way signposted on the right. Follow it across fields towards Hawling. As you approach the village you'll pass the site of an earlier village which was abandoned in the Middle Ages. In strong, low-angled sunlight you can just make out where the houses once stood. There are many deserted medieval villages in this region; some were abandoned because of the difficulty of making a living, or perhaps because of the plague, but others were deliberately cleared by the monks who owned so much of the land and preferred their sheepwalks uninterrupted by villages. Then in 1755 the process began by which the open downs were enclosed with the stone walls which we now think of as characteristically Cotswold. The grid of small fields around Hawling was created at this time.

Reaching a junction with a green lane, you turn right to continue the walk. First, however, it's worth detouring to the left into remote, unspoilt Hawling, one of the highest (and coldest) of Cotswold villages and set in rather bleak sheep country, a part of the Cotswolds once described by Sydney Smith as "a region of stone and sorrow". Hawling comprises church, manor house, Wesleyan chapel, village hall (formerly a school) and a scattering of farms and cottages. The church, dedicated to St Edward, is of Norman origin but was rebuilt in 1764 and restored in 1873, while the manor house is Elizabethan.

Resuming the walk, just go straight on along the bridleway, which is part of an ancient road along which multitudes of travellers and great flocks of sheep must have passed. It was one of the main drove roads to the big sheep market of Chipping Campden.

After about a mile it brings you to a road. Leave the Windrush Way, which makes a left turn here, and continue on the bridleway, which takes you past Roel Hill Farm. Peaking at 960ft. (292 metres), this is one of the finest sections of the walk, with extensive views across the wolds. When the track bends to the left keep straight on instead, with the field boundary to your left.

About a mile from Roel Hill Farm you'll reach a lane at Deadmanbury Gate. Turn left, then take the second right – the bridleway, not the footpath, to rejoin the old drove road. This section is still known as Campden Lane. It climbs gently at first then gradually descends towards a farm. Reaching a lane, turn right, walking past woodland, a large pond and a lovely cottage at Pinnock Warren on the edge of Guiting Wood.

Look for a gate into the wood and join the Wardens' Way, following it straight on through the wood towards Guiting Power. The wood is a large and ancient one, in places a beguiling mixture of ash, oak, beech and wych elm, but with large numbers of less welcome larch, poplar and spruce. Castlett Stream, a tributary of the Win-

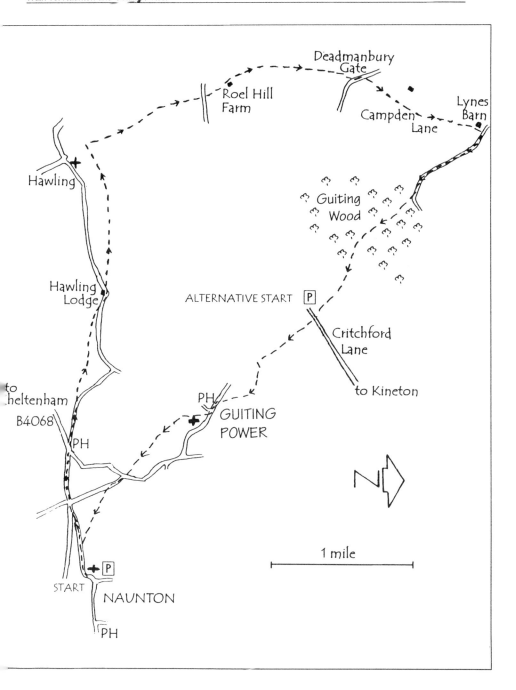

Deadmanbury
Gate

Roel Hill
Farm

Campden
Lane

Lynes
Barn

Hawling

Guiting
Wood

Hawling
Lodge

ALTERNATIVE START P

Critchford
Lane

to
Cheltenham

B4068

to Kineton

PH

GUITING
POWER

PH

N

1 mile

START P

NAUNTON

PH

drush, carves an attractive valley round the wood's northern and eastern perimeters. On leaving the wood follow a sunken lane then continue across park-like pasture before turning left into Guiting Power, a lovely village at the junction of two streams.

The village centre consists of unspoilt cottages surrounding a green but it's well worth exploring the side streets as well. The manorial estate (including about 50 houses) was bought in the 1950s by Raymond Cochrane who placed most of the houses in the Guiting Manor Trust, a charity created for the purpose of restoration and modernisation. In 1977 it was replaced by the Guiting Manor Amenity Trust. The houses are let mainly to local families (from Guiting Power, Temple Guiting, Naunton and Hawling) and preference given to young couples who might otherwise be driven out by high prices. When you're ready to leave, rejoin the Wardens' Way by Watsons' Stores and follow it to St Michael's Church on the edge of the village. This Norman church was partly rebuilt in the 13th century and the Perpendicular-style tower was added in the 15th century. Unfortunately, St Michael's underwent a rather heavy-handed restoration in 1903 but it does retain some Norman work. The foundations of a Saxon chapel have recently been discovered close to the present church and it seems that the original settlement was on this site, but in 1330, when a market licence was granted, the focus of the village moved to the Square.

After leaving the church behind it's simply a question of following the waymarked path across fields to a road. Go straight on, soon joining another path on the left which leads directly to Naunton.

Walk 17: Kingham and Adlestrop

An easy circular walk with interesting literary connections in the Vale of Evenlode. There are no gradients to speak of, the footpaths are easily followed and there are only about 8 stiles.

Start/finish: Kingham Station, grid reference 257226.

Length: 10½ miles/16.8km.

Maps: OS Landranger 163, OS Pathfinder 1068, OS Outdoor Leisure 45.

Refreshments: Pub, hotel and shops in Kingham.

Buses: Pulham's Stow to Cheltenham via Kingham, Thursdays only; Pulham's Bourton and Stow to Banbury via Kingham, Thursdays only; Villager Oddington and Stow to Witney via Kingham, Tuesdays only. Other infrequent local services also operate, provided by Baker's, Pulham's and Villager, but for most visitors the train is by far the best option.

Trains: Thames Trains and Great Western operate daily services to Kingham on the Cotswold Line.

Parking: The car park at Kingham Station is for rail users only but some roadside parking is available round the corner, towards Kingham, opposite Langston Priory. There is also a space between the phone box and the church at Daylesford.

Kingham is an attractive, spacious village on the Oxfordshire side of the Evenlode, a tributary of the Thames. It lies off the main through roads and tends, therefore, to escape much tourist attention.

Leaving Kingham Station, which is some distance from the village, turn left beside the road then soon left again at a junction. As you walk along you can't fail to notice a tall, pinnacled church tower to the east. This prominent local landmark is at Churchill and was built in 1826. The tower is a replica of that at Magdalen College, Oxford, though considerably smaller.

As you approach Kingham you will see an access track on the left to Trigmoor Wood, a Woodland Trust nature reserve. It occupies the site of a former railway junction where the still extant Worcester to Oxford line met the long dismantled Chipping Norton to Stow line. It's well worth exploring, but what a shame there is no direct access from Kingham Station as the reserve extends almost to the edge of the platform.

Resuming the walk, just continue along the road into Kingham, soon taking a footpath on the left which cuts across a green in front of St Andrew's Church, a 14th-century building which has suffered heavy Victorian restoration. Just beyond the church is a group of attractive old houses, including the splendid Old Rectory, dating from 1688.

Continue along the lane to pass Conygree Gate Hotel then turn left on Cozens Lane. At West Street go left again on West End. This is a particularly attractive corner of the village, with lovely cottages in shades of grey and russet. A number of the gardens are bordered by up-ended stone slabs instead of hedges or fences, a feature of the Evenlode Valley which is not seen elsewhere in the Cotswolds.

Turn right by a lime tree on a lane that becomes a wide, hedged bridleway running between fields towards Daylesford, whose church spire is visible ahead. The bridleway takes you to a railway bridge, at which point you should leave it for a footpath, turning right along the edge of a field to reach the road at Daylesford. This attractive estate village is grouped at the start of the driveway to Daylesford House, which stands, unseen from the road, on the hillside above. Daylesford House was designed in 1787 by Samuel Pepys Cockerell for Warren Hastings, born in 1732 at nearby Churchill. Hastings went to India in 1750 as a clerk with the East India Company but later became Governor General of India. He was impeached for corruption in a trial which dragged on intermittently over seven years before he was finally acquitted. It had been a boyhood dream to buy back land at Daylesford which had belonged to his family since the Conquest until it was sold at the end of the 17th century. Though the trial took most of his savings, he was able to acquire the estate and lived there until his death in 1818.

Turn left along the road, passing St Peter's, an elaborate Victorian church, rebuilt in 1860 to the design of J.L. Pearson, architect of Truro Cathedral. Warren Hastings is buried in the churchyard.

Continue along the lane to meet the A436 and cross to a bridleway opposite, next to the lodge which guards the entrance to Adlestrop Park. The bridleway follows a curving route across parkland to

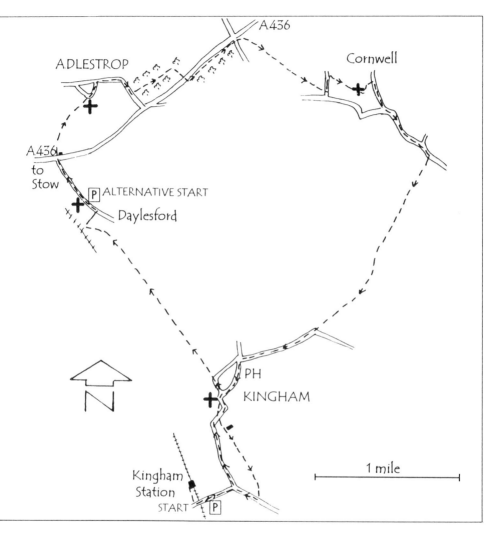

bring you to the edge of Adlestrop, a small, quiet village. This is the loveliest part of it, a harmonious group of houses clustered around the church, which was much restored and rebuilt in the 18th century.

The Adlestrop estate has belonged to the Leigh family since the time of Elizabeth I. The novelist Jane Austen was related to the Leighs and her letters reveal that she made at least three visits to

Adlestrop House

them at Adlestrop Rectory (now Adlestrop House) in 1794, 1799 and 1806. Her mother, before her marriage, was Cassandra Leigh, a first cousin of Thomas Leigh, Rector of Adlestrop and second cousin to James Leigh of the Manor House (now Adlestrop Park). Thomas and his sister were godparents to Jane's siblings Henry and Cassandra. Jane was a keen walker and must have wandered the lanes and footpaths to visit neighbouring villages such as Daylesford, where Warren Hastings was a friend of the Leighs and a great admirer of Jane's novels.

Jane's 1806 visit provided inspiration for certain scenes in Mansfield Park. Sweeping changes to the estate which the Leighs had made on the advice of Humphry Repton appear in the novel in the guise of work carried out on Compton, which was likewise improved by Repton. Thomas also received the news that he had inherited Stoneleigh Abbey, the family seat in Warwickshire, and Jane and her mother went with him to inspect it. The magnificent estate proved a suitable model for Sotherton in the novel.

Edward Thomas also gave the village a measure of fame in his poem *Adlestrop*, inspired when the train he was travelling on stopped there unexpectedly one June day shortly before the outbreak of the First World War. The station, opened in 1853, was closed in 1962, but its old brown and cream GWR nameplate was rescued by the villagers and erected in a wooden shelter, together with a platform bench bearing a plate inscribed with the poem. Thomas saw only the station; he never returned to visit the village but was killed in action in 1917.

Having visited Adlestrop church, continue along the lane to a junction. Turn left here if you want to explore the rest of the village, including the railway memorabilia mentioned above. Otherwise, turn right and then right again when you reach the road, which climbs steadily to the top of a rise before making a right turn. Join the second footpath on the left, which runs straight ahead through a narrow belt of woodland. At the end of the trees go through a gate and follow the right-hand edge of a narrow field to the opposite corner, where another gate gives access to more woodland. The path leads to a road, where you turn left.

Walk along a wide verge beside this pleasant road, which is bordered on both sides by woodland. When you come to a crossroads, leave Gloucestershire for Oxfordshire, turning right then immediately left onto a bridleway which cuts through a wood to emerge on the edge of fields. Go more or less straight across the first field, aiming to reach the far hedge just to the left of a young plantation. Pass through a gap in the hedge and continue in the same direction, beside the tall hedge which borders the plantation. Ahead of you now is a long ridge on which the town of Chipping Norton sprawls prominently, while closer to hand is the village of Cornwell, towards which you are heading.

Go through a gate at the bottom of the field and continue down another field, bearing slightly left away from the hedge to reach a gate to a paddock. Go forward to enter Cornwell, a picturesque village tucked quietly away in this little valley below Chipping Norton. The village was discovered in a run-down state by a wealthy American woman in 1938, and she subsequently bought it, engaging Clough Williams Ellis, the architect who built the bizarre village of Portmeirion on the Welsh coast, to restore it for her. Sadly, her English husband was killed while serving in the RAF and neither of them ever lived at Cornwell.

Turn left until you see a footpath on the right and a sign directing you towards the church. Follow a track until it swings left, and go straight on instead, then diagonally across an orchard. A combination of signposts and stiles now directs you past Cornwell Manor to St Peter's Church, a small, simple building with a bellcote, a sundial, Perpendicular-style windows and some entertaining carved heads.

Follow the path round to the far side of the churchyard, go through a kissing gate and straight ahead to a lane. Turn right and shortly left at a junction with a road. Turn right at the next junction then join a bridleway, also on the right. This hedged, green lane runs straight ahead between fields to emerge on the main road near Kingham.

Turn right and walk through the village. Soon after passing the church join a footpath on the left which passes to the right of the Mill Hotel then crosses a succession of fields, a tributary of the Evenlode and the course of the dismantled Chipping Norton to Stow railway before emerging on a road. Turn right, then first left to return to Kingham station.

Walk 18: Seven Springs and Elkstone

A varied and moderately strenuous circular walk in hilly country, with good footpaths and about 20 stiles. One of the finest Norman churches in the Cotswolds is visited close to the halfway point.

Start/finish: Seven Springs, south of Cheltenham, at the junction of the A435 and A436; grid reference 968171.

Length: 11 miles/17.6km.

Maps: OS Landranger 163, OS Pathfinder 1089.

Refreshments: Pub at Seven Springs, pub and shop at Colesbourne.

Buses: Stagecoach Stroud Valleys 51 Cheltenham to Cirencester and Swindon via Seven Springs, Monday to Saturday.

Trains: Nearest station is Cheltenham.

Parking: Lay-by on the A436 at Seven Springs, just south-west of the junction.

Seven Springs, an upwelling of spring water beside the A436, is the source of the Churn, a tributary of the Thames, and claimed by many as the real source of the Thames (rather than Trewsbury Mead, near Kemble). Sadly, it's a rather tatty, litter-strewn site, nothing to get too excited about, but it is a convenient starting point for this walk if you arrive by car. If you do, then just walk the short distance north to the road junction, which is the starting point for those arriving by bus.

Close to the junction stands a most unusual survival: a small, thatched roundhouse which was built in 1840 for people to leave parcels for collection by the passing carrier, who called daily.

The Walk

Cross the road with great care to join a bridleway (the Cotswold Way) on the east side of the A435. The bridleway climbs gently to reach a lane, where you turn left. Ignore a footpath on the right and then another footpath and bridleway (Cotswold Way to Wistley Hill) branching off on the left. Go left at a junction by a cottage at Upper Coberley then pass through an unsigned, open gateway on the right, just after the cottage, to join a bridleway which runs across a field and then plunges into Pinswell Plantation. Keep straight on until you reach a junction by an isolated cottage. Turn right here to follow the bridleway along the outer edge of the plantation.

When you reach a lane the bridleway continues opposite, running along the edge of Forty Acre Plantation before emerging into sheep pasture. Turn right and follow the waymarked route to Colesbourne. Reaching the road, turn right past the Colesbourne Inn then cross the road and fork left on a lane.

Soon after passing Penhill Farm the lane bends left and begins a gentle climb up the flank of Pen Hill. On reaching a junction, fork right past a triangular green then go straight on at a crossroads. When you reach a row of sycamores, join a footpath which passes to the right of them then continues on a clearly defined route, bounded by a strip of woodland on one side and a young plantation on the other, before it returns you to the lane.

Turn right along the lane but only for a few paces before joining another path on the right which runs along a valley, quite soon turning left at a junction and following a brook towards a patch of woodland. Just before you reach the wood the path climbs slightly to a junction where you keep straight on, with the wood to your left. The path soon bends to the right and a little further on another path is indicated on the left. Take this one, which leads to a junction between two clumps of beeches. Go through the gate opposite and cross a field to a lane. Turn left past The Millhouse into the isolated village of Elkstone.

Cross a green to enter the churchyard and visit the church, dedicated to St John the Evangelist. The Cotswold region is nationally renowned for its Norman churches and this is one of the finest of all. The tower and some of the windows were added in the 15th century, but the basic structure of the church dates from about 1160. As you approach from the green the first feature to strike you will be the unusual east window with its battlemented ornamentation, thought to be unique. The space above this window is occupied by a very rare feature, a columbarium, or dovecote (no longer in use) created when the roof of the chancel was raised to the same level as that of the nave. Another fascinating aspect of the exterior is a corbel-table with

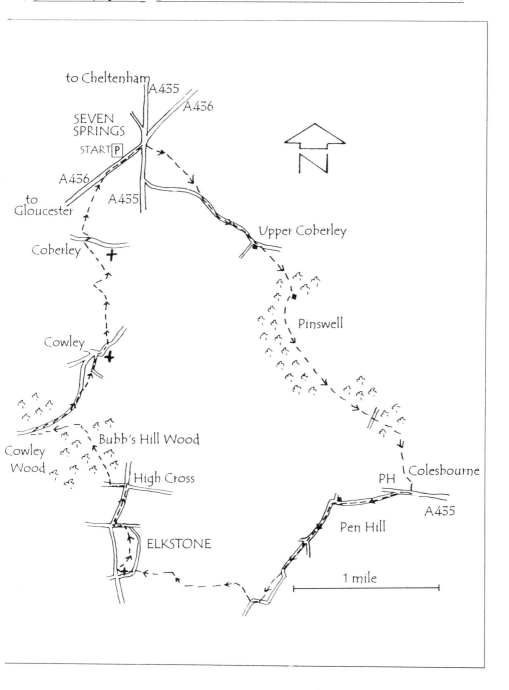

Elkstone Church

carved figures representing mythical, human, animal and bird subjects. Above the south door and protected by the porch from weathering is a superb carved tympanum which is considered to be one of the finest in the country. The interior of the church also contains much of interest, most notably the superb Norman chancel arch with its elaborate chevron carving. A door in the chancel gives access to the columbarium.

Outside the church again, there are some fine 17th-century table tombs similar to the more famous ones at Painswick. By the south-east corner of the churchyard is the Priest's House which dates from the 14th century, though most of what survives is later, including Tudor and Jacobean. Unfortunately, there is not much else to see in the village which, full of new buildings and barn conversions, resembles an enclave of suburbia. There are, however, at least two very fine older houses, both of which you will see if you leave the churchyard by a gate behind the tower. To your left, fronting the main road, is Elkstone Manor, and to your right, at the end of a driveway, is The Old Rectory, with its fine Queen Anne façade.

Cross the driveway and climb a stile into a paddock, joining a footpath which takes you straight ahead along the edges of several fields, guided by a succession of stiles until you are confronted by a tall cypress hedge. Turn left here, walking round a garden to a road.

Turn left to a crossroads then turn right. At High Cross turn left and then join the first footpath on the right, passing a barn and timber-yard then descending beside a stone wall until a stile gives access to Bubb's Hill Wood.

Go straight on along a waymarked path which descends, steeply in places, to a junction with forestry roads. Turn right, then left, passing the end of a pool as you join a bridleway. Emerging into a field, go straight on, with Cowley Wood to your left, until the bridle-way joins a lane. Turn right along here, climbing gently with another wood, Harcombe Bottom, on your left.

Soon after the immense, imposing bulk of Cowley Manor first comes into view, climb a stile on the right into sheep pasture and head towards the manor. A stile returns you to the lane and you turn left to a T-junction, then right. Pass the entrance to the manor, which is now a community care centre and nursing home. It was built origi-nally in 1674 but rebuilt between 1858 and 1860 in the Italian style for Sir James Horlick, co-inventor, with his brother, of the famous drink.

When the road bends right go straight ahead on a footpath. A stile soon gives access to a field. Cross this and the next one then turn left along the edge of a third field to a gate in the corner and go forward to a brook before turning right. A footbridge takes you over the brook and you go straight on across a field to a stile to a green lane. Cross to a footpath opposite which goes diagonally left to the village of Co-berley. Turn right and you'll see a "no through road" on the left near the post office – this is the way back to Seven Springs but those who wish to visit St Giles's Church should keep on along the lane for a short distance. Access to the church is through a doorway in the wall of a barn adjoining Coberley Court.

From 1066 until 1458 the manor of Coberley was held by the Ber-keley family but since then it has passed through many hands. The church was rebuilt in the 19th century but its much older south chapel and Perpendicular tower have survived. The South Chapel was endowed and built by Sir Thomas de Berkeley around 1340 and it contains some interesting 13th- and 14th- century memorials to the Berkeley family, including Sir Thomas, who fought at Crécy, and his wife Joan, who was, by her next marriage to William Whittington of Pauntley, the mother of Dick Whittington, born in 1359.

There is a monument in the sanctuary of a knight holding a heart, commemorating the burial here in 1295 of Sir Giles Berkeley's heart, the rest of his body having been buried at Little Malvern. Heart burials were common enough but this seems to be the only known example in the Cotswolds. In the churchyard a grass mound reveals the burial place of Lombard, the favourite horse of Sir Giles.

Return to the village and join the "no through road" near the post office. It takes you past an unusual sundial erected as a memorial to Queen Victoria. Soon after this the road becomes a bridleway. Keep straight on at two junctions, joining a footpath at the second one. This leads directly to the A436 and Seven Springs.

Walk 19: Kingham to Moreton-in-Marsh

A superb linear walk embracing two small towns, four villages and two hamlets, giving a real insight into that harmonious combination of built and natural landscape which makes Cotswold special. Though longish, it's not too strenuous, with gentle gradients, well-defined paths and only 11 stiles.

Start: Kingham Station, grid reference 257226.

Finish: Moreton-in-Marsh Station, grid reference 206327.

Length: 13 miles/20.8km.

Maps: OS Landranger 151 and 163, OS Pathfinders 1043, 1044, 1067 and 1068, OS Outdoor Leisure 45.

Refreshments: Pubs, tea rooms, restaurants, take-aways and shops in Stow and Moreton; pubs and shops at Bledington, Oddington, Broadwell and Longborough.

Buses: For details see Walks 6, 15 and 17 but note that services to Kingham are very poor and the train is by far the best method of transport for this walk.

Coaches: National Express 511 Great Malvern to London via Moreton, daily.

Trains: Thames Trains and Great Western operate daily services to Kingham and Moreton on the Cotswold Line.

Parking: Kingham Station or Moreton Station.

Leaving Kingham Station, turn right towards Bledington, which occupies the west bank of the River Evenlode and is the most easterly village in Gloucestershire. When you come to a lovely old mill by the Evenlode, join a footpath behind it and follow it into a pasture. Turn left to reach the road then turn right into Bledington, a large village remote from the main through roads which cross the Cotswolds and relatively undiscovered by tourists.

Turn left on Church Lane, which is lined with some lovely houses and leads to 12th-century St Leonard's Church, a beautiful building further enhanced by its setting, with open country to the south and west, and a row of mellow cottages opposite. Even by Cotswold standards this church is quite special. Both Norman and Early English work survives, but much of the best of St Leonard's dates from the 15th century when the church, like so many others in

The village green, Bledington

the region, benefited from the wealth generated by wool. It has a fine set of Perpendicular windows including a clerestory containing some outstanding stained glass. There is a wall painting on the west wall of the nave, dating from either the 12th or 13th century, discovered in 1926 by a churchwarden and restored in the 1980s.

Having admired the church, walk along a quiet back street to the green, around which most of Bledington's older houses cluster. Bordered by a popular pub and bisected by a tributary of the Evenlode, the green is frequented by contented ducks. Some of the surrounding houses have garden fences of upright stone slabs, a feature of the Evenlode Valley.

Walk on beside the main road for a short distance, towards Stow, until you reach a byway on the right. Join this lovely, tree-lined route which leads to Oddington, over two miles away. For the first quarter of a mile the wide verges and ancient, species-rich hedges bordering the byway are protected as a nature reserve created by the parish council. The reserve extends as far as the dismantled railway which once ran from Chipping Norton to Stow.

The byway makes several sharp turns but it's impossible to go wrong if you ignore all the lesser paths which branch off it. After passing through woodland at Bledington Heath and Lower Oddington Ashes, the byway emerges from the trees at St Nicholas's Church, though Oddington itself is still some way off. The first Oddington, a Saxon settlement, was situated here but had been abandoned by the 18th century, leaving the church stranded alone under the trees.

St Nicholas's is surprisingly grand in scale, perhaps because the Archbishop of York had a residence at Oddington in the 13th century and Henry III was a frequent visitor. On the north wall of the nave arcade is a 14th-century Doom painting, which has survived in unusual detail and was restored in the early 1970s. It is one of the finest surviving representations of the Last Judgement. Trumpet-blowing angels summon the dead from their graves and lost souls are propelled by devils into Hell. Some of the torments of the damned are depicted, with one man suspended from a gibbet while others boil in a cauldron with grotesque monsters in attendance. Though some of the details are horrific, the painting is great fun.

After inspecting the Doom, continue to Oddington, an elongated village with a number of 17th-century houses. A peaceful place today, it's hard to imagine that in the Civil War it was the scene of bloody fighting in which the Royalists under Prince Rupert suffered a major defeat.

Turn left along the main street, through both Lower and Upper Oddington. Soon after passing a pub you should notice waymarks indicating that you're on the Macmillan Way. Keep alert for the point at which this makes a right turn, leaving the street. Follow a fenced path then bear left across a field to a stile. Don't cross the stile, but turn left by the hedge until it turns a corner, then go diagonally left across the field to its far corner.

Pass a raised reservoir and keep forward to pass behind a rugby club then turn left to the road. Turn right and continue to a junction where you turn left on a lane which climbs towards the hamlet of Maugersbury. Turn left when you reach it, then right at a crossroads, leaving the Macmillan Way to pass Maugersbury House, Monks Barn and Little Broom.

Maugersbury is a quiet hamlet which enjoys pleasant views from its hillside position and has some very attractive 17th-century farmhouses. It's soon left behind as you arrive on the edge of Stow, the highest town (750ft./229 metres) in the Cotswolds. Head for the town centre, which is based around The Square, where Stow's famous horse fairs and sheep markets used to be held. At the height of the wool trade as many as 20 000 sheep might be penned in The Square on the average market day.

Stow sits at the meeting point of eight roads, including the Roman Fosse Way, but it was already on the route of a prehistoric ridgeway long before the Romans arrived. Centuries before it became a market town Stow's purpose was to provide food and lodging for travellers, a tradition which has never faltered. In the 18th century the King's Arms had the happy reputation of being the best inn between London and Worcester, and there are still numerous inns and hotels today.

The church, tucked away almost out of sight despite its impressive Perpendicular tower, was originally founded around 870, when it was dedicated either to St Edward the Martyr or to a local character, Edward the Hermit (nobody really knows which) but in the 14th century it was rededicated to Edward the Confessor, just to add to the confusion. In 1646 St Edward's suffered considerable damage when it was used to house 1000 Royalist prisoners after a Civil War battle, fought nearby.

Until the 16th century Stow-on-the-Wold was known as Edwardstow or Stow St Edward and belonged to Evesham Abbey. It was granted its weekly market in 1107 by Henry I, though it was another two or three centuries before the Abbot of Evesham was granted the right to hold a fair in the town. Horse fairs continued until the 1980s when they were moved to Andoversford as they were considered to generate crime.

The Square is still the bustling centre of town and is surrounded by pubs, tea shops and old coaching inns. A number of walled alleys lead into The Square and may once have helped direct sheep towards the market place. The remains of a green can be found in one corner, with the town stocks still in place. The heart of town is marked by the restored 14th-century market cross.

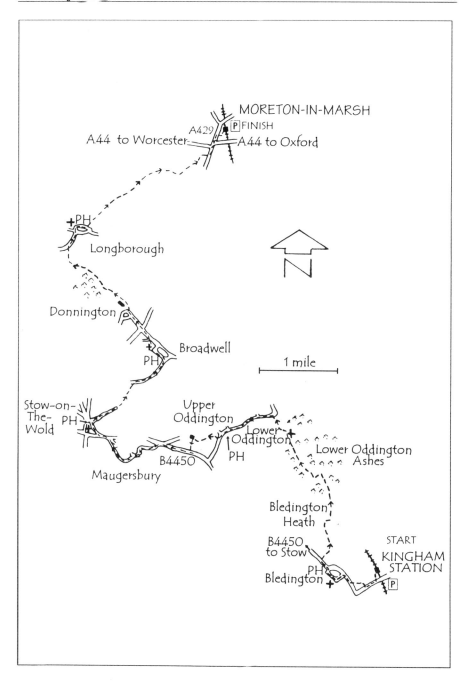

MORETON-IN-MARSH

A429

P FINISH

A44 to Worcester

A44 to Oxford

+PH

Longborough

N

Donnington

Broadwell

PH

1 mile

Stow-on-
The-
Wold   PH

Upper
Oddington

Lower
Oddington

Lower Oddington
Ashes

B4450

PH

Maugersbury

Bledington
Heath

B4450
to Stow

START

KINGHAM
STATION

PH

Bledington

P

Stow is full of interesting buildings, with the Crooked House thought to date from 1450, though most are of the 17th and 18th centuries. Probably the most lovely is St Edward's House of c1730 (not to be confused with St Edward's Hall, which is Victorian) and the oldest is the Royalist Hotel, which claims to be England's oldest inn, founded in 947. Radio-carbon tests have dated its beams to the late 10th century. It lists "leper holes" and "witches' marks" among its attractions.

When you're ready to move on, walk north along the High Street to the police station and the main bus stop, then turn right on a lane at Parson's Corner. Follow the lane to a junction and turn left on Well Lane, a "no through road". There are good views across the Evenlode Valley as you walk along here. The road becomes a track and waymarks indicate you're now on the Donnington Way.

When you reach another lane, turn right and descend towards Broadwell, a quiet village loosely spread around a spacious green beneath Broadwell Hill. The green is one of the largest in the Cotswolds and was formerly a common on which the villagers grazed their animals. The stream along its northern fringe is bordered by willows and by damp-loving flowers in spring and early summer.

Turn left through the village, passing the green and the Fox Inn. When the lane bends right, join a footpath to St Paul's Church. This fine building probably dates from around 1150 and a fair bit of Norman work survives among later alterations and additions. In the churchyard is a particularly impressive collection of 17th-century wool bale tombs – table tombs with rounded tops said to represent corded bales of wool. The yew tree on the south side of the church is thought to be 1300 years old.

Pass through the churchyard to another lane, turn right, then immediately left, towards Donnington and Moreton. Go straight on at a crossroads. These slopes between Donnington and Stow were the scene of a battle in 1646.

At a junction by a barn turn right, and at the next bend in the lane join a bridleway signposted to Longborough. You're now in the hamlet of Donnington, pleasantly sited on a slope overlooking the broad Evenlode Valley, with several very attractive 17th- and 18th-century farmhouses and cottages in an informal grouping. (The famous Donnington Brewery is over a mile to the west.)

Follow the garden wall of Donnington Manor, then go through a gate and forward a few paces to another. Go through and turn left around the edge of a paddock to a wooden gate in the left corner. The waymarks indicate that you're now on the Monarch's Way as well as the Donnington Way.

Go diagonally right to the far corner of another field, through a gate and on along a clear track which leads to the edge of Longborough, where you join the Heart of England Way. When you reach a tarmac lane keep straight on into Longborough. Turn right at a junction and along the main street to a T-junction. Turn left, then right, soon passing St James's Church. This was begun in the 12th century and for a long time belonged to Hailes Abbey. The west tower was built in the 13th century in Early English style but the battlemented and pinnacled top with its eight gargoyles was added in the 15th century, replacing an earlier pyramidal roof. On the right-hand jamb of the porch door is a fine scratch dial, a sort of primitive sun dial for determining the times of the seven services of the church day.

Keep going along the street until you come to Bean Hill. Turn left on a footpath signposted to Moreton. Climb a stile to a field and bear right on a well-trodden path to another stile. Turn left to the far end of another field then go right to cross a footbridge beneath an ash tree. Turn left across a field to a stile then across another field to a footbridge. Turn right to the far corner, go through a gate and then just keep straight on, following the waymarks, which eventually direct you left, to the edge of Moreton. A right turn then takes you to the Fosse Way. The town centre is to the left.

Walk 20: Kemble to Stroud

A long linear walk, beautiful but effortless as there are no hills and very few stiles. The dominant features are woodland and the disused Thames and Severn Canal. Please note that one path (Sapperton Broad Avenue) is concessionary and officially open only from 0800 to 1700 daily. Dogs are not welcome on this path.

Start: Kemble Station, grid reference 985975.

Finish: Stroud Station, grid reference 849051.

Length: 14 miles/22.4km.

Maps: OS Landrangers 162 and 163, OS Pathfinders 1113 and 1133.

Refreshments: Pub at Coates; pubs and shops at Chalford and Brimscombe; pubs, cafés, tea rooms, restaurants, take-aways and shops in Stroud.

Buses: Alex Cars/Andy James Coaches Chippenham, Malmesbury and Cirencester to Tetbury via Kemble, Monday to Saturday; Cirencester to Bath via Kemble, Tuesdays only; for details of buses to Stroud see Walk 14 and for buses to Tetbury (to connect with Alex Cars/Andy James services to Kemble) see Walk 10. If you wish to shorten this walk, Stagecoach Stroud Valleys 22, 26, 28, 29 and 54 operate to Stroud from Coates, Sapperton, Chalford and Brimscombe, Monday to Saturday.

Trains: Great Western and Wales and West operate daily services to Kemble and Stroud on the Paddington – Swindon – Gloucester – Cheltenham line, and some services also operate direct to/from Worcester.

Parking: At Kemble Station or Stroud Station.

Kemble is the first village along the course of the River Thames and a place with a long history, but it wasn't until the 19th century that it achieved any particular significance when it became a busy railway junction. With the closing of the branch lines to Tetbury and Cirencester, Kemble is a junction no more, but the station, designed by Brunel, has recently been restored and for the first time in years something of its former style can be appreciated.

The Walk

Having admired the station, walk to the main road and turn left (unless you wish to explore the village, which is to the right). After a few paces cross to a footpath on the right. Follow the right-hand field edge to another field then continue forward, to the left of an embankment which used to carry the branch line to Cirencester. Very soon you come to a footbridge where you turn left on the Thames Path (don't be surprised to find the river bed is dry). The path soon veers left, away from the river towards the left-hand field boundary then leads to a gate. Keep going in the same direction beside the hedge, but before you reach the end of the field bear right, aiming for a group of trees close to overhead power lines. Steps and a stile give access to the Fosse Way.

This area is known as Thames Head but the actual source is still a little further north, at Trewsbury Mead. Cross to a footpath almost opposite and keep roughly straight on, aiming for a church tower and soon walking to the left of a line of field maples. Reaching a gate and stile bear right to the spring which is reckoned to be the source of the Thames. This is the end of the Thames Path, and for those who have followed this national trail from London there may be a sense of anti-climax for there's nothing much to see, just a shallow depression ringed by stones beneath a large ash tree. An uninspiring stone slab nearby officially marks the spot.

The Thames Path may have come to an end but the right of way continues forward and is easily followed. A wooded embankment on your right betrays the course of the disused Thames and Severn Canal and before long you'll come to Coatesfield Bridge, a small stone bridge spanning the canal. Turn left just before the bridge to join the former towpath. The canal is dry at this point and trees have taken root in it, while a dense growth crowds in on the towpath, with species such as elder, hawthorn, hazel, ash, spindle, wild rose, traveller's joy, ivy, bramble and blackthorn.

The Thames and Severn is one of two disused canals which are often known as the Cotswold Canals. The first to be built was the Stroudwater Navigation which opened in 1779, linking Stroud with the River Severn at Framilode. The Thames and Severn Canal, constructed by a different company, linked Stroud with the River

Thames at Lechlade, thus completing the first ever link between our two greatest rivers. It was completed in 1789, when it was hailed as a stupendous achievement, but its working life was short, thanks to problems with leakage, water shortages and an excessive number of locks. Competition soon arose from the Oxford Canal, opened only a year later, which provided a better link between London and the Midlands, and then, in 1800, the Grand Junction Canal. In 1876 the first steps towards abandonment of the Thames and Severn Canal were taken when the Great Western Railway bought it to prevent any rival company building a track along its course.

When you pass under the railway note the skilful brickwork in the underside of the skew bridge, a small masterpiece of its type. A little further on you pass a three-storeyed roundhouse, one of five built along the towpath in 1790 and 1791 as homes for the canal lengthmen (maintenance men). After this point the canal bed is largely cleared of vegetation and there are long stretches which contain water. Beautiful beech trees overhang the towpath as you approach Tarlton Bridge. Once under the bridge, the next section is known as King's Reach after a visit by George III in 1788.

Very soon, Coates Portal is reached. This classically styled entrance to Sapperton Tunnel was restored in 1977 by the Cotswold Canals Trust, a registered charity whose long term objective is to restore navigation between the Severn and Thames. As well as restoring the two canals, the trust is keen to promote use of the towpath by walkers.

Sapperton Tunnel was completed in 1789 and runs for over two miles to Daneway. When it was first built it was the longest tunnel in the country, and it still ranks third. There is no towpath through the tunnel and boats were propelled through by leggers, who lay on their backs and "walked" the vessel through using their feet on the tunnel roof.

Steps lead up to the 18th-century Tunnel House Inn, where you turn right, then left on a footpath. The path leads into Hailey Wood, which is part of the Bathurst Estate and open to the public, along with Oakley Wood, Overley Wood and Cirencester Park, a huge area altogether and one in which there are very few rights of way, making the provision of concessionary access even more valuable.

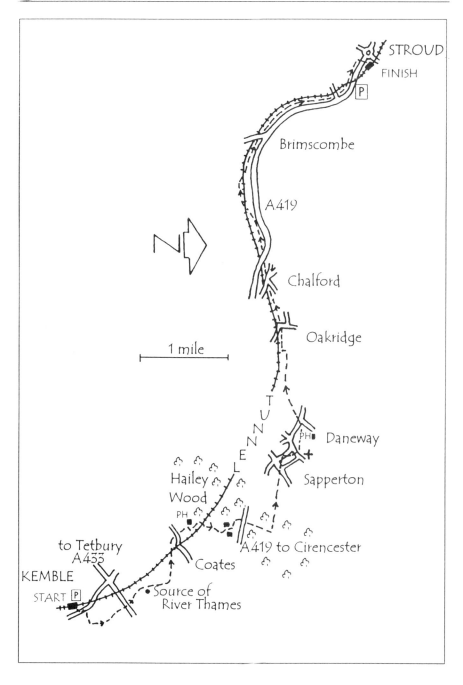

When you come to the railway, fork right to pass underneath. Go right again at the next two forks then as you approach the edge of the wood turn left. Pass through the premises of a sawmill and turn right along the access road for a little way then left on a waymarked footpath. After 300 metres a path branches left – look closely on the right and you'll see a faint one there, too. Join this, and soon fork left to reach the main road. Cross and gain access a little to the left by a blue sign which welcomes walkers to the woods of the Bathurst Estate. Stay on a surfaced ride, ignoring all branching paths, and follow it to a large clearing known as Ten Rides because that number converge on it. Turn left on a broad, grassy ride known unsurprisingly as Broad Ride or Sapperton Broad Avenue. A glance to the right at this point reveals the tower of St John's Church 3½ miles away at Cirencester.

When you find your way blocked by a pair of locked gates, look for another gate on the left and make a brief detour to regain the same heading. On reaching a road cross over and continue along the ride to another road.

Turn right towards Sapperton, a small, grey village beautifully situated on a slight ridge overlooking the wooded Golden Valley, a name which seems appropriate enough in the autumn, but apparently refers not to any scenic quality but to the wealth generated by the cloth industry.

Many of the cottages in Sapperton were designed at the beginning of the century by Ernest Gimson and the Barnsley brothers, craftsmen who were inspired by the Arts and Crafts Movement established by William Morris. The emphasis of this was on the use of traditional designs and materials, and the houses built in Sapperton, such as Beechanger, Upper Dorvel House and the Leasowes, are hard to distinguish from much older ones.

When you reach the green take a path on the right which leads past cottages to another lane and the school. Turn right then take Church Lane on the left. Just after passing Ivy Cottage, turn left on a walled path which leads to a stile. Bear left on a well-worn path across a damp cattle pasture, descending to another stile. Steps lead to the Daneway Portal of the Sapperton Tunnel, which is quite different from its counterpart at Coates, more Gothic than Classical, with an embattled parapet. It was restored by the Cotswold Canals Trust in 1996. Turn right to join the towpath, passing the ruinous remains of a lengthman's cottage to enter a Gloucestershire Wildlife Trust reserve.

Sapperton Valley Nature Reserve is part of a complex of superb wildlife sites in the valley which also includes Siccaridge Wood and Daneway Banks reserves. A mile in length, it includes a stretch of canal bordered by woodland and water-meadows, with the River Frome forming most of the southern boundary. The canal is largely silted up, with reeds and a variety of other vegetation in the more open parts.

Leave the reserve at a stile and continue along the towpath to the road, passing the Daneway Inn. Formerly known as the Bricklayers' Arms, it was built in the 1780s for the men building the canal tunnel, and later catered for the bargees and leggers who worked the canal. The pub car park is built on the top lock of the long flight which took the canal up the Golden Valley.

Turn right then cross to another footpath signposted to Chalford. This takes you back into the GWT reserve as you rejoin the towpath, passing the remains of locks. On your right is GWT's Siccaridge Wood, noted for its wild flowers and birds.

Before long a footbridge takes you across the canal but continue in the same direction through jungly woodland, luxuriantly green with hart's-tongue fern. The River Frome pursues a parallel course on the left. At a brick bridge leave the reserve and ignore a branching path to the left, continuing on the towpath. After leaving the wood behind and passing a number of houses you come to another footbridge. Cross but stay on the towpath, quite soon coming to a most beautifully sited watermill, with a dovecote in its gable wall.

Ignore a wooden footbridge on the left and continue forward on the towpath. The Frome is now on your right as you enter Chalford, where former clothiers' and weavers' houses rise in tiers up the steeply sloping north bank of the valley, linked by a dense mesh of winding lanes and tracks which were once trod by ponies and donkeys carrying great bales of wool and woven cloth or panniers crammed with coal. The mills in which the weavers worked still line the canal, though now converted to other uses.

Emerging on the main road, cross over and join an unsigned footpath opposite, passing a factory and turning right in front of another one to rejoin the towpath. You soon have to rejoin the main road but only for a short distance. Cross a lane and bear left on another footpath which takes you through an area known as Black Gutter and past a roundhouse and the impressive Belvedere Mill. The roundhouse is probably the best example of the five associated with the canal.

There is a much more urban quality to your surroundings now, but it's a landscape full of interest nonetheless. Having passed through a tunnel to go under the railway look out for a GWR cast iron boundary marker just to the left of the towpath. After this you pass through the area known as Blackness where river, canal, railway and road all run parallel. As you approach Brimscombe Mill you need to turn right, left to regain the footpath, then right again to the road. Turn left and very soon left again, opposite a bus stop, back on to a footpath. This takes you to another road. Cross over and pass to the right of the Ship Inn and past Brimscombe Mills.

The Thames and Severn Canal at Stroud

Much of the industry is left behind as you proceed away from Brimscombe, and the canal once again takes on a more rural character which prevails right up to the very edge of Stroud town centre. The River Frome keeps you company too, on and off, while the canal remains an almost constant companion, except where it briefly disappears underground near Brimscombe and again by the bypass on the edge of Stroud. You have a choice of places to leave the canal, such as by the Waitrose supermarket,or at Wall Bridge for Stroud Station.

More Cotswolds guides from:

A YEAR OF WALKS: The Cotswolds
Roy Woodcock

These 12 circular walks, one for each month of the year, visit a range of locations in the Cotswolds. The month-by-month approach encourages you to walk in harmony with the changing seasons . Especially enlightening for local walkers, the book gives new experience and insight to a popular region. £6.95

Due in 1999:

LITERARY STROLLS IN THE COTSWOLDS
Gordon Ottewell

A collection of 40 short strolls with special appeal to lovers of literature and landscape. All less than three miles in length, the routes spread across the Cotsold countryside and encourage strollers to find out more about the area through the discovery of its many-faceted literary associations. £7.95

BEST TEA SHOP WALKS IN THE COTSWOLDS
Norman & June Buckley

No other area in Britain has as many tea shops as the Cotswolds. This book of 26 walks takes the reader the length and breadth of the area, visiting the popular towns and tiny villages. The walks average 5-6 miles and each features a tea shop that welcomes walkers. £6.95

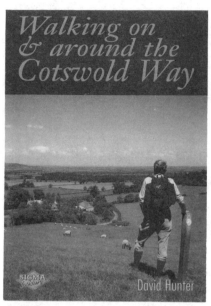

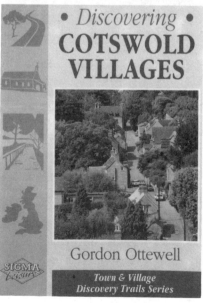

BEST PUB WALKS IN THE COTSWOLDS
Laurence Main

The Cotswolds provide many excellent walking opportunities, plus the chance to discover its unique and characterful pubs. Let Laurence show you around! *£6.95*

WALKING ON & AROUND THE COTSWOLD WAY
David Hunter

There's no need to tackle the whole of the Cotswold Way with this series of stimulating circular walks. 15 routes with excellent maps and photos - the leisurely way to walk "The Way"! £6.95

DISCOVERING COTSWOLD VILLAGES
Gordon Ottewell

"Here, in one compact book, is a practical guide for all those who wish to visit - and explore- the most attractive villages in the Cotswolds. Read about the villages, find out about their history, then enjoy one of 50 pleasant walks to uncover the intriguing past of these... settlements". WORCESTER EVENING NEWS. *£6.95*